Hong Kong, Macau and Taiwan

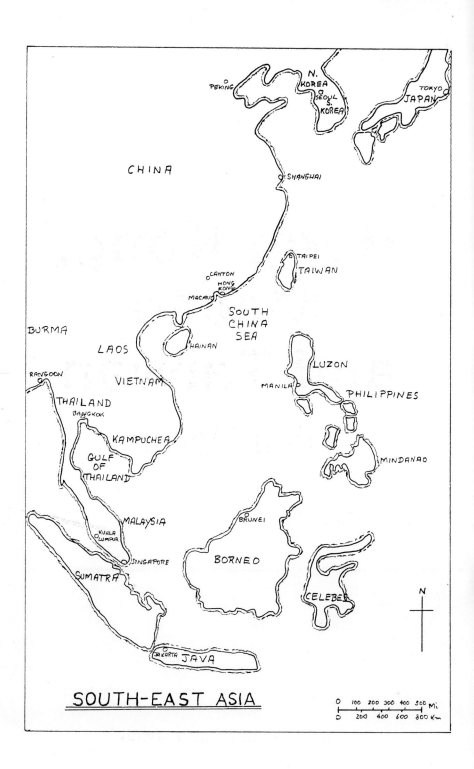

SOUTH-EAST ASIA

Hong Kong, Macau and Taiwan

Nina Nelson

B.T. Batsford Ltd, London

To Harry and Grizel Stanley whose devotion to the Chinese and their way of life inspired me to write this book.

First published 1984
© 1984 Nina Nelson

ISBN 0 7134 3831 2

Phototypeset in Monophoto Baskerville by
Servis Filmsetting Ltd, Manchester
Printed in Great Britain by
Butler & Tanner Ltd, Frome, Somerset
for the publishers,
B T Batsford Ltd,
4 Fitzhardinge Street,
London, W1H 0AH

Contents

List of Illustrations

Reached by a shuttle ferry from Shum Wan pier, the Jumbo can
seat 2500 people   p. 38, 39

24   Carrots are not just carrots to a Chinese chef. After a bit of work they become birds or dragons. The eyes in the carved carrot dragon on the left light up with power from a small battery hidden inside the vegetable   p. 107

Colour

Maps

Line Drawings

Acknowledgements

I owe a debt of gratitude to Harry Stanley without whose encouragement and knowledge this book would not have been written. I am also grateful to the Hong Kong Tourist Association and Government Office Press Sections in London and Hong Kong who smoothed my path in many directions and checked some sections of the book. Special thanks also to Paul Hoskins who helped plan my Macau visit. Once again, Harry waved his magic wand to open up Taiwan and Yu Wei, the Director General of the Tourism Bureau, was most informative and enthusiastic. Anna Chiang, of his staff was indefatigable in ensuring that we saw as much as possible in the available time. Spencer Moosa the writer and scholar who lives there, placed his encyclopaedic knowledge at my disposal.

I was lucky enough to meet Constance Langley and John her husband when they were resident in London after moving from Hong Kong where she was born. If any references to cooking are wrong it is not her fault, but mine.

Others who shouted encouragement from the touch line and kept me up to the mark include Jeffrey Rayner of Intercommunication (PR), Peter French, Tim Reid, Ross Clark, Tony Cocklin, Geraldine Pitt and Pauline Ho. My editor at Batsford, William Waller, who knows Hong Kong has been helpful throughout.

For personal kindnesses and considerable broadening of my knowledge, I am indebted to General Bill Macfarlane and his wife Helen. I would also like to thank the following for kind permission to reproduce their photographs: the Hong Kong Tourist Association for nos. 8, 9, 10, 11, 12, 14, 15 and of the black and white photographs and nos. 1, 2, 3 and 6 of the colour plates; the Hong Kong Government Office for black and white nos. 2, 3, 4, 5, 16, 18, 19, 20, 21, 22, 23 and 24; British Caledonian Airways for black and white no. 1; the Royal Hong Kong Jockey Club for black and white no. 13; the

Macau Tourist Information Bureau for black and white no. 27; and the Taiwan Tourist Office for black and white nos. 17, 33, 36 and 37 and colour plate nos. 8, 9 and 10. My husband, Tony, is responsible for the remaining photographs and drew the maps and Antonia Embleton did a splendid piece of word processing from my paste-ups. The cartoon on p. 21 is reproduced by kind permission of 'Jak'.

1 Hong Kong Background

'How did you like Hong Kong?' asked one traveller of another. 'Exhilarating', was the reply, 'but it will be nicer when it is finished.'

There is no equivalent of *manyana* in Hong Kong. It is jokingly said that at any given moment 50 per cent of the island is under construction or destruction, and sites are changed overnight. During the last decade an amazing city has come into being and it expands all the time. Its population of more than five million is constantly on the go, and enjoys it. It has become the third largest commercial centre in the world after London and New York, and, due to the time difference, while they are asleep, Hong Kong is awake. If all the cars in Hong Kong were on the road at the same time, bumper to bumper, there would be insufficient length of road to accommodate them. Among these cars would be 500 Rolls Royces, the highest density per capita in the world.

Like Holland, Hong Kong constantly reclaims land from the sea. Schiphol Airport some 13 feet below sea level surprises passengers when they see ships above them on nearby canals. Kai Tak Airport astounds tourists when they land amongst the shipping on the runway jutting out into the harbour after flying over mountains and skyscrapers on the run in. It is certainly an exciting landing and Concorde must have been a dramatic sight when she first skimmed in.

Space is not just reclaimed from the sea but through the sea under the harbour in the form of the new Metro. This undersea system, costing some HK $5 billion, is a convenient shuttle service, not only for local people but also for tourists, wanting to cross the harbour quickly. It joins Hong Kong Island Central District to Tsim Sha Tsui in Kowloon. The method of construction was unusual. Instead of boring through the rock below the sea bed, huge tubes were built up in sections, towed into position by tugs with their ends sealed and then sunk and welded together on the sea bed. Now, for a small sum, you can travel quickly between Hong Kong Island and Kowloon and the system is being extended at ground level into the New Territories.

Horses too are involved in this maximum use of available space. Adjacent to Happy Valley Racecourse another building nestling into the mountain side had its roof almost alongside a space used for exercise. By bridging the gap between the two, its area was extended and you can now see horses on the roof.

There are forty-five daily newspapers devoted to news alone – the majority of them in Chinese, three in English and one in Japanese. The press is not subject to any form of government censorship and is free to publish anything, subject only to limitations set by the laws of libel. There are numerous other newspapers for those with special interests, such as music, entertainment, sports, racing and even sex. Official figures show that Hong Kong has the second highest newspaper readership in Asia, after Japan, with some 350 copies of newspapers printed for every 1000 people. The literacy rate is very high, and the press acts as a public forum for Hong Kong people, who do not have an electoral system of government.

Much has happened since Hong Kong became a British Crown colony less than a century and a half ago. Queen Victoria could not have known when she is supposed to have remarked 'Albert is much amused at my having got the island of Hong Kong' that it was destined to be one of the brightest jewels in the British crown.

Long before Hong Kong was ceded, many English companies, including the British East India Company had visited Canton and, following in the wake of Portuguese, Spanish and Dutch traders, set up factories along the Pearl River. These warehouses were just inshore as foreigners were forbidden to go inland anywhere near the imperial walled city. Another proviso was that they had to leave as soon as the winter shipping season was at an end. Those who did not return to their countries spent their summers in rented accommodation in Macau. Profits were excellent but there was one fly in the ointment: in return for tea, exquisite silks and porcelain, the Chinese insisted that payment had to be made in silver bullion. Obviously this presented many difficulties until the British traders thought of an easier trading currency – opium. This was procured in India and shipped to Canton. Less silver bullion swelled Chinese coffers and more opium came ashore where certain officials were inclined to turn a blind eye to the drug in return for 'squeeze money' – a term still used in Hong Kong today. Naturally the Chinese Emperor was not pleased at this turn of events. In 1839 opium was outlawed but continued to be smuggled in. Finally an emissary, Commissioner Lin

Tse-hsu, was sent to Canton by the Emperor to stop the trading of 'foreign mud', as opium was referred to by the Chinese.

Lin Tse-hsu was determined to carry out his mission. He insisted that all opium should be confiscated and laid seige to British warehouses. Negotiations got nowhere during the next few weeks and eventually Captain Charles Elliot R.N., the senior British officer, promised to surrender some 20,000 chests of opium, which he did, and then returned with his ships to Macau.

In the following June a small British naval force retaliated against the Chinese in the first of two battles which became known as the 'Opium Wars'. Skirmishing led to further negotiations but the lucrative opium trade was not to be given up easily by the traders and the treaty was soon broken by both sides. The second Opium War took place and this time Canton was attacked by the British, forts were taken and walls breached. But Shanghai had to fall and Nanking be threatened before the Chinese went back to the negotiating table. In 1841, by the new Nanking treaty, China agreed to open five of her ports to the foreign 'Barbarians' and to compensate for their losses. In the same year she ceded the island off the tip of Kowloon and Stonecutters Island Hong Kong, to Britain and it became an established British Crown colony and free port. Sir Henry Pottinger, who had led the British force, was to become its first governor. The traders could scarcely believe their good fortune in having Hong Kong harbour. This deep water port was open at both ends so ships could sail on any wind.

Lying at the mouth of the river 90 miles (145 km) from Canton, Hong Kong Island is about 11 miles (17.7 km) long and from 2 to 5 miles (3.2 to 8 km) wide with an area of 30 square miles (77.7 sq.km). Its ridge of hills, the highest of which is Victoria Peak at 1823 feet (556 m) leads down to narrow valleys. Its magnificent harbour, 10 square miles (26 sq.km) and 1 mile (1.6 km) across at Star Ferry, in extent, is one of the world's finest. The gross tonnage handled exceeded all the traders expectations and still does so.

Shops, banks and buildings arose and Hong Kong's capital, Victoria, though the name is seldom used today, stretched some 9 miles (14.5 km) along the wharf-lined harbour. A residential district took shape near Victoria Peak. Previously, wives and children had been forbidden in Canton and either had to live the year around in Macau or remain in Britain.

In 1860 the peninsula of Kowloon up to Boundary Road, though part of the mainland of China, was also ceded to Britain. Later on 9 June, 1898, the so-called 'New Territories', together with some 230 islands and islets, were leased by Britain from China for a term of 99 years.

From the beginning, many Chinese flocked to Hong Kong and one of the early governors was said to have remarked that it was far easier to govern the thousands of Chinese than the few hundred Europeans. The mixture of races has got along together except during one strange incident in 1852 when bread, which the Europeans ate instead of rice, was said to have been poisoned. Many people were taken seriously ill, including the governor's wife, and some died, but the majority eventually recovered and the mystery was never solved.

• Hong Kong's population has ebbed and flowed as a consequence of happenings outside its borders. Before the First World War, when the Manchu dynasty fell, there was a great influx of Chinese. During the 1930s when the Japanese invaded China, hundreds of thousands flooded in so that even before the Second World War housing had become almost impossible.

Hong Kong paid its heaviest price for its existence after the Japanese successfully raided Pearl Harbour. They then turned their attention to the Island and attacked it with overwhelming forces. Hong Kong fell in 1941 on Christmas Day. Internment Camps and hunger went hand in hand and the population gradually dwindled to half a million. Yet such is the swing of world politics that by 1950, when civil war tore mainland China in two, the population of Hong Kong had swollen to two million.

The fifties saw more and more refugees from the mainland. Housing was desparately short and to make matters worse an uncontrollable fire swept away a large shanty town in Kowloon. A crash building programme was the only answer. Simple high-rise flats mushroomed and construction went on day and night, but even so, by the sixties, the influx was such that the authorities had to close the border. Despite this, the population continues to increase, largely with refugees from other warring Asian countries.

Although housing remains the major dilemma in Hong Kong, on the plus side construction of other buildings goes on, much of it with great forethought, designed by internationally-known architects. Hong Kong is rich and nothing is too good for it, even if costly. Concrete and glass are there in abundance but creeping in amongst the modern technology there are signs of classical revival. There is a splendid blend of ancient and modern and old traditional building materials are used in conjunction with time- and labour-saving methods. Bamboo, for example is still used for scaffolding, but instead of binding it together with rope, today plastic ties are much speedier.

Bamboo is in fact, to the Chinese what the camel is to the Arab and the pig is to the Westerner; everything but the squeak is used.

Perhaps one of the most important reasons for Hong Kong's commercial success is that the background of the community is a refugee one. Newspapers show countless pictures of the hopelessness and suffering of refugees worldwide. But they are by definition survivors, the ones who have the determination to get away from the intolerable conditions in which they find themselves, the will to move themselves and often their families in difficult circumstances to what they believe will be a better way of life. Consequently, the Chinese in Hong Kong are hard workers who will toil long hours, often in menial or repetitive jobs for lower pay than their counterparts in the West. Worked hard they may be, but they are happier and better off than they would have been had they stayed where they were. Many Chinese proverbs describe this thinking: 'every blade of grass has its own share of dew'; 'Every doorway has its own sky'.

A refugee has adaptability and the Chinese soon learnt how to exploit the situation in which they found themselves. Chinese tailoring is well known but there were soon too many people involved so someone thought of 'quick' tailoring. Passengers from cruise ships stopping off for a couple of days can have suits, dresses, shirts, indeed most articles of clothing, expertly handmade to their measurements, perhaps within the day. This applies also to jewellery. Statistics show that 60 per cent of the visitors coming to Hong Kong do so mainly for the shopping and 20 per cent of those buy jewellery or have it specially designed. Hong Kong is famous for its export of clothing, jewellery, electronics, watches and toys, but perhaps it is not so widely known that it is also the world's largest exporter of candles – an industry that has flourished since the restriction of electricity during the Japanese Occupation.

The adaptability of the Chinese does not prevent them from being extremely superstitious. Red is believed to be a very lucky colour. Door gods are painted on doors to protect certain rooms. Front and back doors must not face each other down a hallway lest evil spirits hurtle through the house. New Year's Day is a time when the house is completely swept through to rid it of evil. But the most fascinating belief is in *Fung Shui*. All Chinese and most Europeans believe in it and even those Europeans who are inclined to scoff, encourage it 'just in case'. Without it, something may go wrong.

Fung Shui is one of the oldest beliefs held by the Chinese. The words mean 'wind' and 'water' and both these have an effect on property you buy. The *Fung Shui* men have carried on this strange practice for generations and their art has decided where temples and buildings should stand, and even reshaped whole landscapes. A *Fung Shui* man can locate exact sites for buildings, gardens, houses, graves, even offices and shops, and if you follow his advice bad luck will pass you by. He uses a lot of impedimenta such as discs and compasses as in a lesser way, a water diviner uses his dowsing equipment.

We visited Ronald Noel Paton, the Far East Manager for British Caledonian Airways, in his office in the South China Building and noticed that the white Venetian blind was drawn over one window behind his desk. As it seemed a little odd I asked him the reason. 'When we started here 18 months ago,' he said 'I sent for a *Fung Shui* man in accordance with Chinese custom. I expected someone in Chinese dress with a bag of assorted instruments and charms. I was wrong about the dress. A gentleman arrived smartly turned out down to his Gucci shoes, but I was right about the contents of his elegant brief case.'

'What would you have done if he had asked you to change your office?' we asked.

'Fortunately he approved of the office but he said it would bring bad luck if I looked out of that window. I drew the blind there and then and have never looked out of it since. He was also very interested that the British Caledonian logo is a lion as this has great significance for the Chinese. He recalled that Prince Charles had 'dotted' the eye of a processional dragon during his visit to Hong Kong in 1979. He said that, to ensure good fortune for the airline, the inaugural flight should arrive at an exact hour at Kai Tak airport and that a VIP should 'dot' the eye of the lion on the tail fin of the aircraft. Accordingly we instructed the Captain to arrive at the exact time chosen even if he had to circle around the South China Sea for a while! He landed spot on time, we raised the *Fung Shui* man up to the fin of the aircraft on a fork life truck with our Managing Director, Alastair Pugh, who 'dotted' the eye of the lion and business has been brisk ever since.'

Most Chinese are eager to be buried in their place of origin and coffins are sent back to Hong Kong from all over the world. But land prices in Hong Kong are high and burial land is no exception. Most cemeteries lease out ground on a seven or ten-year lease and when the lease expires, the remains are exhumed and cremated. Mount David cemetery, in the north-west of Hong Kong Island, has a Coffin House which has been the home of the dead for more than a century. It consists of three halls, where rows and rows of coffins are lined up neatly. There are also about 100 smaller rooms which are for individual families and each contains one or two coffins. In one of these rooms there is a magnificent coffin which contains the remains of the mother of a multimillionaire who could well afford to buy a suitable burial place. The problem is that the *Fung Shui* man has yet to decide where is suitable!

Almost as soon as Hong Kong became British one of the first things that was thought of for leisure was horse racing. It was difficult to find a suitable site and it was not until the 1840s that a large flat expanse of marshland was drained for a racecourse. Shortly after, horses were shipped in and a two-storey bamboo viewing stand set up for racegoers. So Happy Valley Racecourse was born and it has remained the most popular form of recreation in Hong Kong.

A number of religions are practised in Hong Kong and there is a tradition there that all faiths join together in charitable works. Many Chinese are Christians and there are several churches, but the main beliefs are Buddhism and Taoism. Of the 600-odd temples and monasteries in the territory, over half are Buddhist and many of these are dedicated to Tin Hau, the protector of fisherfolk and Kwun Yum, goddess of mercy. There are also Moslems and Indian Sikhs and there are three Sikh temples in the vicinity of Queen's Road on Hong Kong Island. The Hindus have a temple in Happy Valley and there is a Jewish synagogue in Robertson Road.

Hong Kong's Governor, who is the personal representative of the Queen, is assisted by an Executive Council and a Legislative Council, the latter consisting of both civil servants and private citizens appointed by the Governor and known as 'unofficial members'. For the city there is an Urban Council consisting of six official and twenty unofficial members of whom ten are elected. Administration of the New Territories is in the hands of a District Commisioner assisted by district officers.

The Hong Kong flag is a blue ensign with its coat of arms below the right corner of the Union Flag. The coat of arms has a lion on one side and a dragon on the other guarding the sea, with two Chinese junks breasting the waves.

When you arrive at Kai Tak airport you will notice the smartly dressed, helpful police. The Royal Hong Kong Police Force is more than 22,000 strong and their distinctive uniforms can be noted as they control traffic and go about their duties. Walkie-talkies keep officers in touch with each other and there is also an auxiliary force of part-timers. Those who saw the excellent television series in Britain recently will have some idea of the variety of work they do and the speed of their reaction to incidents. They have a marine division

1 The lion's eye of the first British Caledonian arrival is dotted by the Managing Director, Alastair Pugh, in the presence of the *Fung Shui* man.

covering the huge harbour and some 240 islands with 1300 officers and 45 launches. Some senior ranks are recruited from police forces in the United Kingdom. Specialist squads include those dealing with the Triad gangs, narcotics, commercial crimes and armed robberies. English-speaking constables wear a red patch beneath their shoulder numbers. The Independent Commission Against Corruption, staffed largely by ex-police officers, does exactly what its name implies, with considerable success.

Foreign currency or travellers' cheques can be changed in most shops and all hotels in Hong Kong, although banks and money changers in Kowloon and Hong Kong Island will give you the best rate of exchange. Money changers are usually open at regular trading hours. The unit of currency in Hong Kong is the Hong Kong dollar (HK$) based on the Mexican silver dollar via the Philippines, as it was the only currency acceptable to the Chinese with their love of silver. Coins are issued in denominations of HK$5, HK$2, HK$1, 50 cents, 20 cents, 10 cents and 5 cents. Notes are available in denominations of HK$1000, HK$500, HK$100, HK$50 and HK$10.

The Gold and Silver Exchange, established in 1911, is now the third largest in the world after London and Zurich and there is a closed membership of nearly 200 firms. As with the Stock Exchange the time difference is an advantage to traders as it means Hong Kong can carry on trade when the others are shut.

As much of Hong Kong Island is steep, unproductive hillside, most of the fresh vegetables and fruit come from China and the New Territories which also provide Hong Kong's water from huge reservoirs. Tap water is officially rated as safe to drink. Hotels and restaurants usually have their own supply but, when eating at inexpensive places, it is wiser to order green tea, like the locals, if you do not have wine or beer.

Although many of the old customs and traditions live on in Hong Kong alongside the modern technology, certain things are disappearing. Rickshaws, for example, are now a rarity and the government no longer grants licences for them. You will see some occasionally waiting for people to have photographs taken in them, the drivers hoping to be asked to pose for a tip. Sedan chairs you will only see in museums and some of these are very beautifully carved and painted. Just once in a blue moon you might see a very, very old lady with tiny feet which were bound at birth, but thankfully this strange, barbarous custom ceased many years ago. Neither will you see anyone with the traditionally long finger nails you may have read about. The reasons for them were many: a sign of nobility when one did not soil one's hands with work; the little nail was sometimes kept long it is said to enable you to scratch the back of the neck in a genteel fashion. The wonderful silk hats the mandarins wore had one jewel set in the top denoting rank, but I did not even see one mounted with coral or jaspar which would have denoted a lowly station. No doubt the emeralds and diamonds were taken years ago.

The attractive jackets and straw hats always associated with the Chinese are still worn, however, especially by the boat people. The *Cheong Sam*, the sleeveless dress with a stand-up collar and slit sides, is sometimes seen and still used as a uniform for hotel and restaurant staff. Fortunately this attractive dress is sometimes worn on formal occasions, heavily embroidered and reaching the floor. Jackets and dark trousers can be seen on both elderly men and women in the streets.

The Chinese calendar operates on a twelve-year system. It is believed that the Lord Buddha requested the animals of the world to join him on New Year's Day. Those that would come to pay homage would not go unrewarded. Only twelve animals answered the call beginning with the rat and ending with the pig. A year is named in honour of each one and this cycle is repeated every twelve years. The animals are in order thus; the rat, the ox, the tiger, the rabbit, the dragon, the snake, the horse, the sheep, the monkey, the cock, the dog and the pig.

Although the early spring is usually a good time to visit Hong Kong most experienced travellers prefer the autumn up to about Christmas time or just beyond, for then the temperatures range from 60° to 80° Fahrenheit and there are usually blue skies. From mid February to the end of April humidity is high and the Peak is often hidden by clouds. The typhoon season is the summer time until September.

Festivals are many and colourful and the following list will enable you to arrange your visit to coincide with one if you wish.

February   *Chinese New Year* is the most important festival of the year. Since time immemorial peach blossom has heralded it in. It is a time when families get together to rejoice. All debts must be paid, new clothes are bought. It is virtually the only time during twelve months that shops and businesses close for three days but, being Hong Kong, it is still possible to make purchases. Remember that, during the festival and for nearly a week before, hairdressers and barbers charge double prices. Everything is decorated and firecrackers explode continuously. Gifts and visits are exchanged among friends and relatives. Children receive paper boats and 'lucky money' which they can burn so that ancestors will not be denied any necessity in the afterlife.

Also in February is the *Lantern Festival*, end of the Chinese New Year. Multi-coloured lanterns hang in every house, market and shop.

April *Ching Ming Festival*. People visit family graves, bring food and burn paper money as offerings to their ancestors.

April/May *Birthday of Tin Hau*, patron saint of seafaring people and a most important festival for Hong Kong's 'boat people'. Boats and junks are decorated and firecrackers sparkle over the water. On shore there are lion dances and traditional rites at the Goddess' temple in Joss House Bay.

May *Bun Festival*. This goes on for four days on the island of Cheung Chau to placate the restless spirits of eighteenth-century victims of Chinese pirates. Procession of floats, papier maché effigies and lion dances go on tirelessly. Buns are fastened to bamboo frames some 60 feet high. There are competitions to climb them and afterwards the buns are eaten.

June *Dragon Boat Festival*. Dragon Boats race against each other to frighten away the sharks from the body of a fourth-century statesman who drowned himself to show his disapproval of the Emperor's injustice. Special lunch tours are arranged for people to watch these exciting races. The boats are realistically decorated like dragons with swishing tails.

August *Yue Lan*. Festival of the Hungry Ghosts. Offerings are made to spirits of the dead who are released for one day only from the underworld.

September Gifts of moon cakes, wines and fruits are exchanged. Adults and children go into the parks and countryside at night with lighted lanterns.

October *Chung Yeung Festival*. Large crowds climb the Peak and other hilltops in imitation of a Chinese family who climbed a mountain long ago and so escaped death when their village was destroyed below. It is also a time for refurbishing family graves.

December Although snow may not actually fall on Victoria Peak at Christmas time the whole of Hong Kong joins in the celebrations during the festive season. Their love of merriment is born in them and Christmas is called by the Chinese, 'The Holy Birthday'. The street decorations really surprised us when we were there as we had not thought of Christmas as being a Chinese occasion, despite the large number of them who are Christian. They seem delighted with the idea and the decorations remain in place for the Chinese New Year, so there are two good reasons for their lavishness. They make London's Regent Street look sombre.

2 The Cheung Chau Bun Festival takes place in May and lasts for four days, shaking the whole island to the beat of cymbals, gongs and drums with lion, unicorn and dragon dances. The pillars of the gates here are made out of fresh buns.

3 Three dragon boats racing to victory at Hong Kong's Dragon Boat Festival which is celebrated each year on the fifth day of the fifth moon (in May/June).

Hong Kong Background

There is a blaze of coloured lights and great hoardings with irridescent pictures of sleds, reindeer and figures of Santa Claus carrying bags of gaudy gifts. Streets are crowded with sightseers and people on shopping sprees. Last year a 36-foot high Christmas tree was sent from mainland China and the Canadians contributed two tall firs which were set up in Alexandra House and Connaught Centre. The elevated walkways seemed full of Santa Claus figures smiling greetings above their white beards and, with the temperature well above that in Europe, everyone was in good spirits and not wearing the heavy clothing we take for granted. Every shop seemed to have tape recordings of carols which were sometimes drowned by the noise of the cash register adding up the money from the sales which Hong Kong is clever enough to have *before* Christmas.

It seems every family wants a Christmas tree, not an artificial one but a live one, and one of the daily papers reported that 300 Norwegian spruces were sold before they were even shipped from England. After a six-week journey in refrigerated containers they were delivered to the purchasers but the entrepreneur behind the operation claimed he could easily have sold 300 more. Indeed, more will be going out each Christmas in the future because, despite the fact that they are genuine, they are less costly than artificial ones!

While we were there carol concerts were held in the City Hall and disc jockeys join St. David's Welsh Male Choir and the Salvation Army band for carol singing on the Star Ferry concourse. Several hotels had their own carol singing choirs. To add to the excitement a Father Christmas arrived out of the blue, not with his reindeer, but from a helicopter, to join in the 'Carols for Charity Drive'. Crowds gathered, everyone was very generous and the collection went to the Children's Hospital in Sandy Bay. One evening there was a mini riot as keen amateur photographers jostled for the best vantage points to set up their cameras and tripods to record the scene.

Of the many controversial figures who have admired Hong Kong, Sun Yat-Sen was one who lived in all three places covered in this book; he studied in Hong Kong, practised medicine in Macau and spent his declining years in Taiwan. Son of a Chinese Christian missionary, he was born in 1866 and when he was 21 went to Hong Kong to study at the recently opened College of Medicine. He was its first graduate. Nearly 40 years later when giving an address at the university he said he felt he had returned home and continued:

Because Hong Kong and its university are my intellectual birthplace I have never before been able to answer the question properly but now I feel I am in a position to answer it today. The question is, 'Where did I get my revolutionary and modern ideas from?' The answer is I got them in this very place, in the colony of Hong Kong. I compared Heungshan [where he was born] with Hong Kong and, although they are only 50 miles apart, the difference impressed me very much. Afterwards I saw the outside world and I began to wonder how it was that foreigners, the Englishmen, could do as much as they had done, for example, with the barren rock of Hong Kong, within 70 or 80 years, while in 4000 years China had no place like Hong Kong. . . . Then the idea came into my head, why cannot we do the same thing in China? My fellow students, you and I have studied in this English colony, and in an English university. We must learn by English examples. We must carry this English example of good government to every part of China.

The year was 1923.

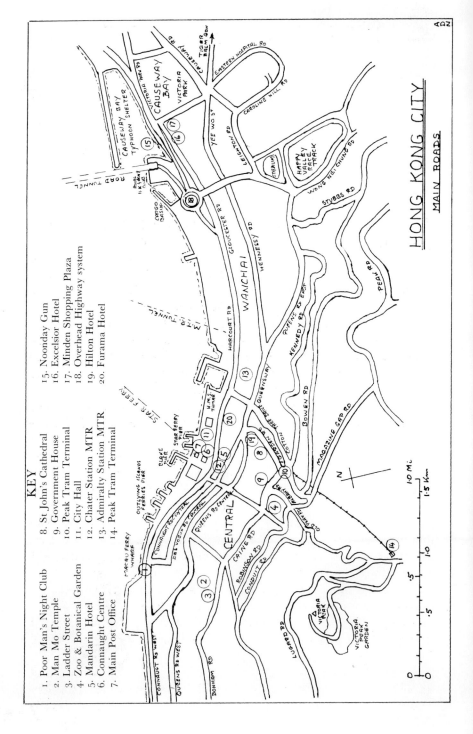

KEY

1. Poor Man's Night Club
2. Man Mo Temple
3. Ladder Street
4. Zoo & Botanical Garden
5. Mandarin Hotel
6. Connaught Centre
7. Main Post Office
8. St John's Cathedral
9. Government House
10. Peak Tram Terminal
11. City Hall
12. Chater Station MTR
13. Admiralty Station MTR
14. Peak Tram Terminal
15. Noonday Gun
16. Excelsior House
17. Minden Shopping Plaza
18. Overhead Highway system
19. Hilton Hotel
20. Furama Hotel

HONG KONG CITY

MAIN ROADS

2 Hong Kong Island

The name Hong Kong means 'fragrant harbour' or 'fragrant waters'. There are various explanations as to how the island acquired this name, depending on which translation you prefer. One goes back to the days of the first settlers who apparently established an incense factory as one of the earliest developments, and the pleasant aroma filled the harbour and greeted boats when they landed there. A different version traces its origin to a waterfall near Sandy Bay which never runs dry, even in drought years, and from which the early sailors are thought to have obtained their fragrant, as opposed to brackish, water. Whatever the story behind it, the name became generally accepted and has remained to the present day.

Nothing is quite as heady as those breathtaking moments when you first glimpse such wonders as the Taj Mahal by moonlight or Niagara Falls floodlit. From the air such sights can be even more striking – the Pyramids as you skim over them going into Cairo airport or circling the temple of Abu Simbel before landing. When our British Caledonian aircraft landed at Kai Tak I caught my breath in the same way. On one side the mountain peaks of the Chinese mainland; then on either side, and even looming above you, the high-rise buildings of the burgeoning cosmopolis, and finally levelling out on the two-mile long runway in the middle of the large busy harbour. I cannot think of any other arrival by air which is quite so dramatic.

The airport itself is situated virtually in the centre of Kowloon, but it is only 3 miles (5 km) from the famous Star Ferry which crosses the harbour to Hong Kong Island, to which the alternative means of travel are a helicopter service, the underground railway or the road tunnel. If your destination is on the island, it can take anything from five minutes to half an hour to reach it, depending on your means of travelling. The deluxe hotels, such as The Mandarin, will send free transport in the form of one of their hotel cars, often a Rolls Royce, to fetch you if you have booked your hotel in advance. Look out for your name on one of the boards held by uniformed men at the airport building exit.

Having heard so often about the immense overcrowding in Hong Kong it is with some surprise that we drove along the wide streets and freeways after our arrival. Even the Cross-Harbour Tunnel, built by Costain, with its bright lighting and fast moving traffic made us feel there was plenty of room. As we emerged onto Hong Kong Island and turned along the shore where the broad sweep of Victoria Harbour was bustling with ships of all sizes – junks, lighters and ferry boats – the air of spaciousness was preserved. After a few minutes drive our car drew up at The Mandarin Hotel.

The Mandarin, from its opening in 1963, rapidly took its place among the leading hotels in the world. In 1981 René Lecler placed it the best in Asia in his guide '*The 300 Best Hotels in the World*' for *Harpers and Queen* magazine and Thomas Cook. It has become a byword among experienced travellers for its cuisine and service, and boasts a ratio of two members of staff to each room. Situated in Connaught Road, in the area known as Central, the heart of the business section, the 25-storey building commands a view of Victoria Harbour. Two hundred yards away is the terminal of the famous Star Ferry to Kowloon and a similar distance to the rear is the Central station of the Mass Transit underground railway which also connects with Kowloon.

The lobby of The Mandarin exudes an atmosphere of grandeur; not surprising when you hear that the decor was done by Don Ashton, scenario designer for the film *Bridge over the River Kwai*. Magnificent Venetian chandeliers hang from the ceiling. Chinese gold carvings decorate the onyx-faced walls. Near the lift hall a slender staircase spirals upward. This takes you to a luxurious shopping arcade. It is connected by footbridges to five other shopping galleries in Prince's Building, Alexandra House, Swire House, Connaught Centre and the Landmark Building, together comprising probably the most expensive shopping centre in Hong Kong.

The 'Chinnery Bar' is also on the first floor and is named after the painter.

George Chinnery, was born in London in 1774 and having made a name for himself in Britain, travelled abroad to document current issues for periodical magazines, as was the habit of artists in the days before photography. Chinnery went to India where his portraits became well-known and then, anxious to avoid his debts and his wife whom he declared was 'the most unattractive woman he had ever

The Standard, September 27

"Usually, we only start with shark's fin soup, but in your honour . . . !"

met,' he fled to Macau. He was witty and eccentric and soon became part of the social life of Macau and Hong Kong. His portraits and scenes of life in both places were much in demand. The walls of the Chinnery Bar are hung with some of his portraits and paintings of Victoria harbour full of old sailing ships. The ambience is restrained and definitely British with deep leather chairs, and expatriates can order their roast beef and tankards of draught beer.

The Man Wah restaurant serves classical Cantonese food and it is advisable to book ahead. A black and gold lacquer screen dominates one wall and sweeping pink silk curtains drop down to a complementary magenta-coloured carpet. The French restaurant, takes its theme from Pablo Picasso's 'Pierrot'. Its luxurious red velvet furnishings and the prints by Picasso and other masters set the mood for traditional French cuisine for lunch and dinner. Adjoining the Pierrot restaurant on the twenty-fifth floor is the Harlequin Bar, with views over Victoria Harbour, Hong Kong Island and the Kowloon Peninsula.

Andreas Hofer, the general manager at the time of my visit, has a Swiss-German background. With his father and grandfather both being hoteliers, inevitably he became involved with the profession, and from the age of 15 thought of nothing else. He has studied or worked in Europe, America and the Caribbean and while still in his early forties he joined the Mandarin, some three years after it opened. It is said that he is as punctual as the Greenwich time signal. Many of his staff have been there as long, if not longer, and he firmly believes that it is not the building which created the Mandarin but the people in it.

Despite the Mandarin's fixation with service they also have a sense of humour. For example, the occasion when Eartha Kitt was performing there in cabaret. She found time on a Sunday to lead a sponsored walk. The management met her halfway with a hamper, complete with ice cold champagne, on one side of which was written 'Eartha's Kit'.

You can see two important buildings from the Mandarin which are only five minutes walk away, the Supreme Court and City Hall. The latter is not an old building in Victorian style as you might suppose but a large modern one facing the waterfront. Hong Kong cultural life has centred around it ever since it was opened in 1962. It contains the local Museum of Art, City Hall Library and a concert hall which can be converted quickly for theatrical productions and seats 1500 people. There is also a smaller intimate theatre, which can be turned into a cinema, lecture rooms and two restaurants and bars. Visiting European companies perform there regularly. Hong Kong itself has both a Philharmonic Orchestra and a Chinese one. Chinese opera, puppet plays and acrobatic performances are held there regularly. All are well advertised in the newspapers.

Close by Statue Square and Chater Gardens stands the Supreme Court building edged with trees and greenery. With its Ionic colonnaded façade and superb white dome it has been a landmark since the beginning of the century, and it looks on the surface as though it would last for many years to come. Unfortunately the construction of the tunnel nearby for the Mass Transit underground railway has weakened its foundations and although engineers have devised means to keep it secure for the moment, this is not a longterm solution. We were talking to a lawyer about this and asked what would happen if it was demolished and replaced by a new one elsewhere. The lawyer shrugged his shoulders fatalistically, then laughed and said: 'In the meantime, thank heavens, I have chambers in Lincoln's Inn in London. So fortunately have many of my legal friends!'

Turning left out of the Mandarin front entrance the first street you come to on the left has the evocative name of Ice House Street. Soon after the colony was founded, long before the days of refrigeration, there was an ice house here, using the principle that ice insulated with sawdust will keep for months. The ice may have come from mainland China. It is a short street containing some elegant shops and when you see the name Asprey you are not mistaken, for it is indeed the first branch to be opened by the world-renowned Bond Street firm. As it is small it cannot carry the full range of goods of the parent firm, but anything can be obtained from London within 24 hours. The shop is on the street level of Prince's building which houses, among others the head office of British Airways and the ticket office of British Caledonian Airways.

Aspreys held a reception in the Connaught Room at the Mandarin to inaugurate the opening of the shop. There was an air of expectancy for many had heard of the scale models of the *QE2*, Concorde and Harrier aircraft in silver. Concorde took a year to complete and had 400 parts, several of which worked. The other two took one craftsman 1800 and 2000 hours respectively to finish. One craftsman above all others who must appeal to lovers of Chinese objets d'art is the one who concentrates upon creating lions in gold. At the exhibition there was an 18-carat gold tea service, worth HK$5 million, originally made for an Indian maharajah, which was sold even before it left the hotel. Leonard Penny, a well-known jewel expert in Hong Kong, is the manager of this new Aladdin's Cave. A gracious host he invited us to dine one night and introduced us to Jack Pearce, Asprey's clock expert.

Well-known in England for his restoration work, Jack had been summoned to Hong Kong from Bond Street to mend a clock of such intricacy it seemed almost impossible. However, before we left we called in at the shop and he demonstrated it to us in full working order. Made by James Cox of London in about 1760 it was one of a pair given by King Christian V of Denmark to the Emperor Chien Lung who was fascinated by European clocks and kept them at the Summer Palace in Peking until they were looted during the Boxer rising. Now restored to its former glory by Jack Pearce, Aspreys had just sold it.

If you walk down Ice House Street and cross Chater Road you will soon come to one of Hong Kong's main streets, Des Voeux Road, crowded with vehicles and with trams in the centre. Tram routes cover a total of 19 miles through some of the world's densest traffic and they are perfect for sightseeing out of rush hours as they are clean and cheap. The great favourite of both residents and tourists alike is the Peak tram which is certainly different from the others, but equally inexpensive. It starts opposite the American Consulate in Garden Road. Although called a tram it is really a funicular railway, running up to Victoria Peak. It is well over 90 years old, carries 80 passengers and the steepest section is 45 degrees. It takes you up 1306 feet (398 metres) in eight minutes to enjoy a marvellous view from the upper station. The Peak tram's first journey was on 28th May, 1888. The Governor and his wife 'were delighted with the charming views of the city and its surroundings which were obtained from almost every point on the route'. In those days there were no roads or buildings on the Peak and people had to be carried in sedan chairs for their picnics.

The distant views are the same today as then, but the foreground is now mostly filled with the high-rise buildings which march up the slopes. On a clear day it is certainly spectacular: the fantastic harbour housing the third largest container port in the world after New York and Rotterdam; the nine dragon hills of Kowloon and the distant mountains of China. At night a carpet of fairy lights is spread below you, the neon signs flicking on and off like glow worms, the ships at anchor reflected in the water. The tram station, which leads into a restaurant and shopping area almost like a small airport, is not actually at the top of the peak but there are roads and a level one, called Lugard Road, takes you for some two miles on a circular walk which is most rewarding, especially if you have a camera. Paths and roads take you higher on to the inevitable radar and radio stations at the top, but there is also the Victoria Peak Garden. If you like peace and quiet it is important to remember that the Peak Tram is terribly crowded during the spring and autumn festivals when the Chinese traditionally go up to the hilltops.

Almost opposite the Peak Tram station, Upper Albert Road runs westward between Government House on the right and the Botanical and Zoological Gardens on the left. Nearby, in Garden Road, is St. John's Cathedral built in grey stone between 1847 and 1849 in Gothic style.

There is no entrance fee to the Gardens and if you visit them before breakfast in the early hours, you will see many people, oblivious of your presence, practising *Tai-Chi*, often called 'Shadow Boxing'. You will find more about these exercises in the chapter on sports and pastimes.

There is a small zoo with different types of monkey, racoons, jaguars and pumas. The aviary is extensive and has one of the best bird collections in the Far East. There are benches and a central fountain. All kinds of sweet smelling flowers such as jasmine and tuber roses grow in carefully tended beds. Sometimes you will see that most lovely of oriental flowers, the lotus, with its pale pink petals. Well cut grass edges pathways and pavilions and there are all kinds of flowering shrubs and trees.

Government House on the opposite side of the road also has lovely gardens which are thrown open to the public once a year when the azaleas are in full bloom. British governors and ambassadors often seem to find it difficult to persuade the British Government that they need a suitable residence in which to receive guests and to entertain. The Governor's residence in Hong Kong has been no exception to this rule, with its unusual background. The first building was blown down by a typhoon a month after it was built. The second served also as offices and, when the first official governor Sir Henry Pottinger arrived in 1843, he had two further bungalows added to enable him to give dinner parties and receptions. He was a tenacious man and spent much of his time complaining to London until finally HK$70,000 was allocated to build a suitable Government House. This took so long that Sir Henry Pottinger had left before it was finished. The building was still not entirely suitable and governors came and went, each complaining in turn. Finally, by 1869, an adequate Government House became the focal point of social occasions and there were receptions, dinners and musical evenings. Eventually Prince Alfred, Queen Victoria's second son, came on a visit and stayed there. However, by the time Sir William Des Voeux became governor, it was again in need of repairs and still did not have a ballroom. Sir William somehow got permission for an annexe to be built and a fancy dress ball was held in 1891 to which the governor's lady went dressed as a swallow.

By the time of Queen Victoria's Jubilee Government House possessed electric lighting and later electric ceiling fans were installed. In later years the ballroom was enlarged and other rooms added. By the 1930s there was talk of a completely new house but this did not materialise and, when Hong Kong was captured by the Japanese, they appointed a governor. General Rensuke Isogai did not approve of several things, especially the fact that an air raid tunnel built underneath it might have made the building unsafe. Obviously he had more control over his Foreign Office because he had the residence rebuilt. The mansion today owes much to him. Although he entertained there he never actually lived in it preferring the Repulse Bay Hotel.

Back to the present day and to the lower level, the Hilton hotel is at the junction of Queen's Road and Garden Road. It has an epicurean selection of restaurants including the Eagle's Nest, a deluxe Chinese one on the twenty-fifth floor with views over the harbour. At the other entrance there is an underground discotheque. The galleries have some 40 shops but perhaps its most unusual attraction is its ship, the *Wan Fu*, a reproduction of the type of brigantine used in the 1840s by the British Navy to hunt down pirates in the South China Sea. She is 110 feet (33.5 metres) in overall length and comfortably fitted and staffed for cruising enjoyment. You can book for two-and-a-half hour cruises for lunches or dinners, barbeques or even island hopping.

A curious lane in the Central district, known as Ladder Street, is literally a street of stone steps leading from Hollywood Road to Caine Road. Its origin is uncertain but reference in an old history book to sedan chairs carrying people up the 200-foot (61-metre) slope to the residential area above, make it at least a hundred years old – a rarity in modern Hong Kong. However, Ladder Street is not alone in this district as one of the older attractions. At its junction with Hollywood Road, it shares the limelight with one of the longest-established temples in Hong Kong – Man Mo, which dates back to 1848. You get the pungent smell of joss sticks when you enter, and there is the glimmer of gold plated sedan chairs which are used for carrying the statues of Man and Mo, known for their military and intellectual skills, around the district at festival times.

The temple faces Hollywood Road well known for its shopping. Here in addition to antiques, porcelain and silver, perhaps because of the proximity to the temple, you will find wreaths, coffins and burial garments. Very often visitors confuse the original Ladder Street with another much-frequented stone stairway not far off in Central District. This is Pottinger Street, named after the first governor of Hong Kong, Sir Henry Pottinger, (1843–1844). It starts close to the waterfront and stretches up to Hollywood Road and there are innumerable shopping stalls on the way.

Upper and Lower Lascar Row is in the Hollywood area and is always known as Cat Street, even by tourists. It is lined with curio and antique shops of every kind with people always milling about for this is the haunt of bargain hunters. The name 'Cat' derives from the diminutive of the now outmoded pidgen English 'catchee' meaning 'to buy', implying a market place.

Wing Sing Street is another place with a nickname – Egg Street – because it is the wholesale centre for the egg trade warehouses on either side. Most of the thousands of eggs sold there daily are imported by train from Jiangsu Province in China. Salted duck eggs' sales soar heavily during the mid autumn festival because they are an

4 Sprawled over the pavement is a selection of the 115 newspapers on sale each day in Hong Kong.

5 Hong Kong's Egg Alley. Decorated with dragons and finely glazed, these egg jars provide extra income to egg wholesalers who sell them to gardeners for potting large plants.

important ingredient of mooncakes which are made by the thousand. These eggs are preserved in large round earthenware jars, some 300 in each. The jars themselves also produce income because they are sold as flower pots for planting seeds for the Lunar New Year. The Chinese believe that flowers blooming at that particular season will bring good luck and prosperity. You will see them as part of the decor in Chinese restaurants in Britain.

Hong Kong's Stock Exchanges, three in number, have world-wide importance. It has always been the banking centre for south-east Asia and during recent years its banks have attained international stature. In particular the Hong Kong Shanghai Bank seems to have the Midas touch. Its building has been a landmark in Central district since 1935. Now it is being replaced by another mightier edifice some 600 feet (183 metres) high, which is expected to be completed by 1985.

A famous pair of lions used to flank the old entrance, one growling and the other with mouth closed but watchful and alert. Passers by used to stroke them for good luck. Looted by the Japanese during the Occupation they eventually turned up in Osaka whence they were returned to their former position. Appropriately enough, while they were being set up, a workman found in one a bullet hole containing some coins. Now while they await their position in front of the entrance to the new building, they have been moved to a place of safety duly prescribed by a *Fung Shui* man.

The new building will have three towers of 41, 35 and 28 storeys. It is to be a steel-framed building, supported by huge girders at the corners of the tower. The street level will be clear giving free passage between Des Voeux and Queen's Road with escalators rising to the first floor banking hall. The ceiling of this hall will be ten floors high and it will be surrounded by balconies on the nine intervening floors. The *Fung Shui* experts did not wholly approve of the original design but the famous British architect, Norman Foster, has incorporated their suggestions into the final arrangement and ensured that the requirements of wind and water are fully met.

After a short while in Hong Kong it is easy to become blasé and take everything you see for granted. It is perhaps worth remembering then that originally Queen's Road was the old water front and all the space between that and the present shore line is reclaimed land. The tall buildings are all standing on deep piling and the busy streets, squares, wharves and sports grounds occupy hard-won acreage. Your visit will be greatly enhanced if you get some of the excellent free leaflets produced by the Hong Kong Tourist Association and go on some of the tours and walks they suggest.

To get an impression of Hong Kong's layout I recommend a harbour trip from Blake Pier near the General Post Office. The landmarks are pointed out to you and the shipping all around is fascinating. Particularly so are the typhoon shelters which are harbours enclosed by breakwaters. They contain lines of Chinese junks on which live the boat dwellers. It is said that some are born, live and die without ever coming ashore. Certainly the boats make a captivating sight with gay colours, window boxes, small children, pets and most of the appurtenances of homelife. Small boats ply back and forth selling vegetables, fruit and anything needed and larger ones supply drinking water and fuel. Perhaps it is fortunate in this instance that the Chinese are generally small in stature.

A ten-minute tram ride eastwards from Central brings you to Wanchai which is one of the main nightlife districts publicised by the legendary Suzie Wong. It is a glitter with neon signs advertising bars and night clubs often 'topless'. So long as intending patrons realise that the soft drinks ordered by their pretty hostess will be priced in the champagne bracket, they are mostly harmless enough while imparting an air of mild wickedness and adventure.

On the other hand why not visit the Poor Man's Night Club. It is a 'happening' which takes place each evening in the area in front of the Macau ferry pier. As if by magic, as darkness falls, the open space is filled with stalls selling cheap merchandise and freshly cooked food. Fortune tellers know all, acrobats perform, music of all kinds blares from loudspeakers and individual groups. Bargains are sought out by visitors and residents alike.

About a mile east of Wanchai lies the prosperous district of Causeway Bay, site of the first British settlement in the 1840s' Jardine Mathieson was the first large trading company to build along the waterfront where their 'godowns' (warehouses) stood for years. Although in modern premises today, they still are responsible for firing the Noon Day Gun which stands in front of the Excelsior Hotel and points in a friendly fashion at the brightly painted yachts moored in the famous Royal Yacht Club basin. It is fired daily at midday out over the new typhoon shelter, and, as it sounds, you will notice that people quickly glance at their wrists to check that their watches are right.

The gun is an old naval weapon, a Hotchkiss three-pounder, and the story behind it is entertaining. Years ago it was the custom to fire a greeting round when naval ships entered the harbour. On one occasion it was fired in error to greet a Jardine Mathieson ship instead of a naval one. As a penance, Jardine Mathieson were ordered to fire the gun at noon each day and they still maintain a two-man private army to do so 80 years later. Arrangements are occasionally made for visiting VIPs to fire the gun, and Major Harry Stanley organised this for Noel Coward on one of his visits. This added to its fame when the Master wrote his immortal piece *Mad dogs and Englishmen*.

Mention of Jardine Mathieson recalls a story told about them at the end of the Japanese Occupation in the last war. A member of the company immediately had one of the strong rooms opened where two cases of whisky had been carefully stored against such an occasion, and toasts were drunk to the defeat of the invaders.

The Excelsior Hotel belongs to the Mandarin group and is a British Airways Associate Hotel. About half its 952 rooms and 30 suites have the spectacular view over the typhoon shelter with its regimented rows of tiny sampans and houseboats. Beyond, in the anchorage, can be seen a cross section of the world's shipping interwoven with junks and fishing vessels.

The Excelsior's night club gives a view even further afield as it is perched some 400 feet above the harbour. There are two Chinese restaurants, three European ones and a British style pub with no inhibitions about opening hours. The Coffee Shop is called The Windmill and is decorated in Dutch style. I thought that the Christmas Day menu over the page from one of the restaurants would convince the reader, should he find himself in Hong Kong on that day, that the Excelsior has a proper sense of tradition.

The Excelsior adjoins the World Trade Centre Club which has tennis courts and a mini-golf practice area and also a large shopping arcade called Yee Tung Village which you can reach from the second floor. This is a Chinese bazaar with some 70 stalls at many of which you can see demonstrations of traditional skills.

If you fancy a handpainted carved bird you can choose between blue birds, bald eagles, snowy owls or mallards at the stall of the wooden bird carver. If you are in the market for a cure for a back ailment or an aphrodisiac, you can buy a deer's tail at the herb stall or perhaps bear gall, said to be a painkiller, and the inevitable *ginseng*, reputed to prolong life even at the deathbed stage. Some Europeans swear by the cure-alls *Pak Fai Yau* (white flower oil) or Tiger Balm ointment. There are craftsmen in calligraphy, jade and ivory carving, steel plate engraving, silhouette cutting and wood block printing. Stalls sell brassware, paper lanterns, sandalwood fans and silkscreen-printed clothes. Food is not forgotten and the aromas will draw you to watch deft fingers making egg rolls on a hot griddle with a bamboo stick; more sophisticated versions containing sesame seeds, coconut or chocolate; or dragon's beard candy, a Chinese version of the familiar candy floss.

6 A junk with the Hong Kong skyline in the background.

PRAWN AND AVOCADO COCKTAIL
or
HOME-MADE PATE
***

CREAM OF CORN
or
CONSOMME WITH MARROW
***

TRADITIONAL CHRISTMAS TURKEY
Giblet Gravy
Rissoles Potatoes
Brussel Sprouts
Glazed Chestnuts
or
SUGAR GLAZED HAM
Madeira Sauce
Sweet Potatoes
Creamed Spinach
***

CHRISTMAS PUDDING
or
MINCE PIES
or
PARFAIT GLACE ST. NICHOLAS
***

COFFEE or TEA

The Excelsior Hotel has its own shuttle minibus service half hourly from 8 a.m. in the morning to 6.30 p.m. to Central and back. You buy your tickets in the lobby. If you cannot make up your mind what food you would enjoy most for your next snack or meal you only have to go out of the hotel entrance to your right. The second turning is aptly named Food Street. It is straight and not very long, and down its centre fountains play, illuminated at night in gaudy colours. It is too narrow for traffic, but wide enough for you to walk from side to side and see what type of restaurant or snack bar you would like to patronise or perhaps book a table for the evening. The Riverside Restaurant serves Cantonese meals. The Siu Siu specialises in light Cantonese snacks, while the King Heung Restaurant features Peking-style dishes, and the Cleveland Restaurant, despite its name, is well known for hot, spicy Szechuan food. In the Dim Sum Restaurant, patrons may sample delicacies from steamed pork buns to spring rolls. Congee noodles are the main attractions at the Phoenix. Japanese-style barbecued steak is a highlight at Hooraiya Teppanyaki, while at the Hooraiya Japanese Restaurant, the menu includes *tempura sushi* and *sukiyaki*.

Again, if you turn right after leaving the front of the Excelsior Hotel and walk past the small entrance to Food Street you will come to Hong Kong's favourite open space – Victoria Park. The park, which is on land reclaimed from the sea, was opened in 1957. It is alive with activity from dawn to dusk and plans have been announced to spend HK$17 million on providing more facilities. Although the park covers only a relatively small area by world standards – 17 acres (7.38 hectares) – thousands of Hong Kong people make use of it.

If you are interested in statistics, about half a million people a year take a dip in the swimming pools, over 80,000 keen young footballers take part in mini-soccer competitions and another half a million attend shows and Chinese operas sponsored by the Urban Council. Thousands more use the tennis courts and others end up sitting down with a bump in the roller skating rink or get themselves quick exercise with a game of squash. Quite apart from all this organised activity many thousands of people from toddlers to 90-year-olds visit the park for a stroll beneath the trees and perhaps admire the plumage of the birds in the small aviary.

In Hong Kong people like to get up early and the park is busy from 6 a.m. onwards with many enthusiasts practising *Tai Chi*. Old men sit beneath clumps of trees, traditionally the type of gathering place for bird fanciers. Their small birds in their bamboo cages are suspended from low branches while their owners discuss the relative merits of plumage and song. There is more about these particular pastimes in Chapter 7.

The more energetic people pound their way around a recently laid 600-metre jogging track ticking off the laps in their minds or counting them with their electronic watches, thus unconsciously advertising that Hong Kong is the biggest producer in the world of this type of watch.

A large statue of Queen Victoria holding the orb and sceptre and seated majestically on a throne whose arms are lion heads is near one of the entrances. She gazes seriously at the skyscrapers up the hillside. Like so many figures of the Queen, it has been through many vicissitudes. When the Japanese invaded the island it was sent to their homeland with others to be melted down for armaments. Somehow it escaped this fate and was returned to Hong Kong from Tokyo in 1946. It faces south in the traditional manner of Chinese Imperial statues.

At Chinese New Year the tarmac mini-soccer pitches are taken over by a colourful flower fair and people flock to the park to buy the small orange trees, peach blossom and flowers that always appear at this important festival.

Within easy walking distance from Victoria Park is Happy Valley, also on reclaimed land, this time not from the sea but from a malarial swamp. Its racing track and the Royal Jockey Club are described in the chapter on sports and pastimes. There are some 60 racing events during the season there and the stands hold about 54,000 spectators. In the same area in Taihang Road you can visit the extraordinary Tiger Balm Gardens created by a millionaire, Aw Boon Haw, in 1935. He invented the well-known ointment Tiger Balm, which was supposed to cure everything from rheumatism to scorpion bites! One section might have been dreamed up in an opium nightmare and is supposed to represent Hell. Although much of the statuary is grotesque there are pleasant pavilions and a striking white pagoda. Rumour has it that the land is to be redeveloped but in some ways this will be a pity.

Flyovers lead traffic high above the crammed shopping street out to the south coast along a twisting, picturesque road through wooded hills. There are many attractive houses along the route and you pass near Deep Water Bay with its fine beach and nine hole golf course on the way to Repulse Bay. This was named after H.M.S. *Repulse* a battleship which helped round up several pirate ships in the early days. The bay has a fine crescent shaped beach with white sand and is enclosed on three sides by green slopes and hills. Flowering trees and shrubs are everywhere so the scene is always colourful even in December when great clumps of red and yellow hibiscus blossoms are at their best.

Then there is the Italian Garden in front of the site of what used to be the Repulse Bay Hotel. This hotel has recently been demolished after a long wrangle with the developers, but in its day, it was famous for its Sunday lunches and 150-foot (46-metre) long verandah, and made history in December 1941 when it was one of the last places to hold out against the Japanese and was beseiged for 72 hours, withstanding frequent sniper attacks.

Further east is the poplar residential area of Stanley, site of a Japanese prisoner of war camp during the 'forties. As manners counted for a good deal in Hong Kong in those days – indeed, they still do – it is said that the Japanese General took the British Governor prisoner with punctilious formality. Four years later when the roles were reversed the same Japanese General was removed with equal ceremony. It is interesting to note that Stanley Village, Stanley Park in Vancouver and Port Stanley in the Falklands all derive their name

7 A tradesman's van about its business among the boat people in Hong Kong harbour.

8 Cable cars at Ocean Park transporting visitors to the Ocean Theatre for performances by trained dolphins and sealions.

from Lord Stanley, Minister of State for the Colonies 1832–1834 and 1841–1845 and, later, three times Prime Minister as the Earl of Derby.

Stanley, once a quiet fishing village, is now a delightful residential spot. It has recently achieved notoriety because of its market. Well-known makes of the latest teenage 'gear' are on sale at amazingly low prices. The more mature visitor will find hand stitched and embroidered linens including tablecloths and mats, counterpanes, handkerchieves and blouses. There are ceramic, jewellery, leather and rattan work stalls offering a profusion of wares. You can easily get to the market by taking a number 6 or 260 double-decker bus from the Central Bus Terminal near the Star Ferry and you will enjoy a scenic ride. If you visit Stanley in the morning there is no better place to have lunch than Stanley Restaurant in the High Street facing the harbour. The most pleasant place to book a table is on the first floor verandah which has a wonderful view seawards.

Who has not heard of Ocean Park in Hong Kong? Opened in 1977, it contains the largest Oceanarium in the world. Non-profit making, it was founded and is managed by the Royal Jockey Club. A cable car takes the visitor on a spectacular journey over Repulse Bay, with views of Aberdeen and many of the islands of the South China Sea. The 170-acre (69-hectare) site covers an entire peninsula. Attractions include a marine theatre with performing killer whale, dolphins and seals; a wave cove with more seals, and penguins and sealions; and an underwater gallery where you can watch 300 different species of fish in their natural habitat. There are altogether some 30,000 fish in this, the world's biggest, aquarium.

It has been said that fishing to live and living to fish have been Aberdeen's way of life for nearly a century. Called after Lord Aberdeen, Foreign Secretary in Peel's cabinet of 1841, tradition survives despite its unlikely name and the influx of tourists. Some 30,000 Chinese live their entire lives on junks. Only in recent years have the floating seafood restaurants, which are famous the world over, made their appearance. Moored in the centre of the harbour, often three stories high, they are painted red with decorations of gold and other colours. At night, when they are outlined by millions of golden lights, their pagoda-shaped top decks make them appear like circus tents. Hundreds of junks and sampans vie with one another to carry you to them. In addition, Aberdeen is a big fishing harbour so there are all the comings and goings of this industry.

The overall effect is of enormous vitality and a scene probably unlike anything else in the world. At sunset things quieten down when people gather together on decks to watch the changing rainbow colours behind the peaks of Lantau Island in the distance.

9 Dolphins in action – they never fail to fascinate audiences at Ocean Park with their hoop act.

10 A water-taxi in Aberdeen's harbour. This is how the boat people travel to and from their floating homes.

11 Dusk brings the lights to life on the Jumbo, one of Hong Kong's famous floating restaurants at Shum Wan, near Aberdeen. Reached by a shuttle ferry from Shum Wan pier, the Jumbo can seat 2500 people.

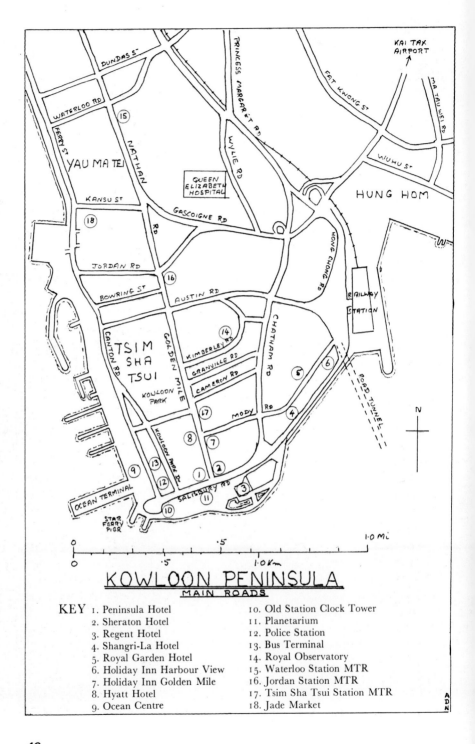

KOWLOON PENINSULA
MAIN ROADS

KEY
1. Peninsula Hotel
2. Sheraton Hotel
3. Regent Hotel
4. Shangri-La Hotel
5. Royal Garden Hotel
6. Holiday Inn Harbour View
7. Holiday Inn Golden Mile
8. Hyatt Hotel
9. Ocean Centre
10. Old Station Clock Tower
11. Planetarium
12. Police Station
13. Bus Terminal
14. Royal Observatory
15. Waterloo Station MTR
16. Jordan Station MTR
17. Tsim Sha Tsui Station MTR
18. Jade Market

3 Kowloon

It is related that long ago the young Emperor Ping, standing on the peninsula across the harbour from the island that was to become Hong Kong, began counting the hills on the island to the mountain range in the distance. 'There are eight' he declared, 'Eight dragons'. The minister accompanying him shook his head. 'There are nine' he said, Ping queried this. The minister bowed. 'Your Imperial Highness is the ninth dragon' was the reply. Dragons are invariably associated with royalty, and so it came about that the peninsula was named 'Kowloon' (nine dragons).

The traditional and inexpensive way to cross the harbour from Hong Kong Island is by the famous Star Ferry. Like those efficient ferries in Scandinavia the ships are spotlessly clean and smart, and all appear as if newly painted. They have two decks for two different classes and therefore load and unload rapidly on two levels. The flow back and forth is continuous and the crossing takes about ten minutes. During that time you can relax on your comfortable seat and watch the pageant of shipping on either side, including hovercraft making the same journey. The ferries operate on other routes as well, including those to the outer islands. If you miss the last ferry at night you can take a 'walla walla' (motorised sampan) which seats some eight or ten people.

When you step ashore in Kowloon you are immediately confronted by the truly vast Ocean Terminal/Ocean Centre complex with four storeys of shops, cafes and restaurants. In Star House is the spacious 'Harbour Village' with its wax museum, more restaurants and stalls where Chinese crafts are produced before your eyes as in the 'village' next to the Excelsior Hotel – even to the candy floss. 'A gift from a distant land will be treasured though it be a swan's feather', so goes an old Chinese saying, and you can certainly find feather dusters, boas and flowers. An expert can write your name in Chinese calligraphy using a distinctive wooden pen, and have the characters incorporated into a dragon and phoenix design suitable for framing. Mr Yip Lai Chuen can be consulted on astrology and palmistry. You can buy traditional cloth buttons, porcelain vases, tea sets in wicker baskets, wooden jewellery chests, brass wall plaques, exquisite paper cuttings, paintings and scrolls. Much of the decor is green and you sense its hypnotic effect until perhaps someone mentions food. Then you might suddenly realise you are hungry and that back in Ocean City there is what is called the 'World's Largest Restaurant'!

Ask Jimmy Wu how many people he can seat for dinner in his restaurant complex and his first estimation will be about 8000, 'but it will be 10,000 when everything is opened', he will add. If you walk around the restaurants, night clubs, snack and cocktail bars you begin to believe him. The whole complex covers over 150,000 square feet and includes a night club which can seat 1500 people. Bearing in mind that most of the food served is Chinese and that Hong Kong diners demand fresh food straight from the kitchen, you wonder how it can be done. 'Oh, about 400 people work in the kitchens,' says Jimmy casually, 'and another 400 or so as waiters and waitresses.' Everything is served from *dim sum* to an 'imperial feast'! For the latter, costing at least HK$6000, 14 gourmets can sit down to a menu which includes 'double-boiled wild duck with fish maw soup and longevity herbs', 'braised snow bear's paw with ham', 'braised superior crown shark's fin', 'chrysanthemum crackers' and 'deluxe moon fairy pie'.

Also adjacent to the ferry terminal is the last trace of the original railway station of the Kowloon-Canton railway – the clock tower alone has been left standing. The new railway terminus is about a mile to the north-east on reclaimed land and, judging by its size and layout, seems to have been built in anticipation of great things to come. It is much larger than is needed for the present number of trains which run on the 22-mile route to the border.

After you leave the Star Ferry and turn right by the Kowloon Post Office into Salisbury Road, at its junction with Nathan Road you will come to the Peninsula Hotel. It celebrated its fiftieth anniversary in 1978. It is a gracious building in the shape of an E without the central section, the open side enclosing a courtyard with fountains and facing the harbour. Built in the twenties when there was no shortage of space, it is not overshadowed by highrise buildings nor does the Space Museum recently built in front of it intrude in any way.

When the Peninsula opened on the 11th December 1928 the *South China Morning Post* hailed it as 'the finest hotel in the Far East – the building itself one of the largest in the colony.' At that time the railway station was close by and it served as the station hotel. Hong Kong was the eastern terminal of the Trans-Siberian railway and there was a service from here to the French Channel coast via China, Siberia, western Russia and northern Europe which took 14 days. A year after the Peninsula opened, the Duke of Gloucester was the first member of the royal family to stay there. Its fame spread, the number of guests increased and fashionable functions such as the annual St Andrew's Ball were held there. The famous and infamous arrived not only to see but to be seen.

Inevitably, with the coming of the 1939 war, business slackened and the sad day came when it was the scene of the formal surrender of Hong Kong. Sir Mark Young, the Governor, was placed in custody in room 336. When the Japanese had gone after the war the Peninsula was requisitioned by the Hong Kong government for office space and quarters, and it was not until the end of 1946 that it came into its own once more as a hotel. Leo Gaddi, who like so many famous Swiss hoteliers started as a chef, was at that time manager at the Palace Hotel in Shanghai. He was offered the post of manager of the Peninsula. He accepted, and the hotel, like a phoenix, came back to its old splendour. In 1952 at the coronation of Queen Elizabeth II its whole façade sparkled with thousands of golden lights. The open-air verandah was enclosed in glass at a cost of HK$26,000 and is one of the city's favourite eating places. The lobby with its high gilded ceiling and ornate pillars remains one of the 'in' places to eat.

Leo Gaddi was to remain at the helm of the Peninsula for some 30 years and the hotel's best known restaurant, 'Gaddi's', is named after him. Many international gourmets consider it the best continental restaurant east of Suez. The cuisine is predominantly French with a fine selection of wines including a large range of vintage champagnes and rare chateau-bottled clarets. Colours are pastel, emphasised by gilding. The *pièce de resistance* is a priceless seventeenth-century Coromandel screen, lent by Sir Lawrence Kadoorie. It depicts the Emperor K'an-Hsi and his court in his summer palace being entertained by dancers. It stands nine feet high with twelve eighteen-inch panels extending across the entrance to Gaddi's Bar.

The Space Museum and Planetarium building opposite the Peninsula Hotel is shaped outside like a gigantic white meringue. It has lecture and exhibition halls and is claimed to be the most modern and largest in the world. Certainly you begin to feel almost like an astronaut when you enter the Sky Theatre, its many projectors showing films simultaneously aided by some 300 additional projection devices. The constellations you know are all there, the sun, moon and more besides. All move around and above you realistically, so that it is almost with relief that you come down to earth again at the exit.

Nathan Road branches off from Salisbury Road with the Peninsula Hotel on one side and the Sheraton on the other. It is Kowloon's principal artery and, together with the roads branching off it, the colony's largest shopping district. Visitors from all over the world come here to buy, and millions of dollars change hands on buying, wining, dining and entertaining. The road stretches some three miles ending in Boundary Street, past the residential district known as Kowloon Tong, at the point where the New Territores begin. The road, dating back to the turn of the century, was laid out as an avenue by the governor at that period, Sir Matthew Nathan. A tree-lined throughfare, some 100 metres wide, it was known as 'Nathan's Folly' because, at that time, the area was not built up and the few people who lived there thought it unnecessary and a waste of money. No-one thinks that today, although unfortunately the trees have disappeared in most places.

The Sheraton Hotel has a rooftop swimming pool and bar and from there you can get a good idea of the city's layout for, although Kowloon is not as large as Hong Kong Island, there are about twice as many people living there and building constantly goes on. Despite this, Kowloon Park, edging a section of Nathan Road, is still inviolate and there is a pleasant vista of Victoria Harbour.

The Great Wall Bar in the Sheraton just off the lobby is a popular place to relax after shopping. Behind it is a unique wooden mural of China's Great Wall carved by a well-known local artist, Cheung Yee. Another unusual feature of the Sheraton is the bullet shaped lifts of anodised metal, two of which operate on the exterior wall of the building while the third is internal and serves the hotel's own shopping mall as well as all the other floors. Going down in the outer lifts is rather like descending by helicopter. The Brussels Sheraton has the same device. Because most shopping is duty free it is wise to remember what is not, and the two items that affect tourists directly are alcohol and cigarettes. However, the Airport Duty Free Stores department has four downtown outlets in addition to those at Kai Tak: at Hotung House in Kowloon, in Ocean Terminal called The Wine Cellar, in the lobby of the Hyatt Regency and in Minden Plaza at Causeway Bay. If you decide to postpone your purchases until you pass through the airport duty free lounge on departure you should realise that you may pay more than you would have done had you bargained in the ordinary shops.

As well as thousands of small shops there are several department store chains such as Shui Hing, Wing On, Sincere, Evergreen, Da Da and Klasse. The most upstage one is probably Lane Crawford which has three large shops, one of them in Nathan Road. There are dozens of tailoring shops, one of the favourites being Sam's, hidden at the end of a small gallery called Burlington Arcade off Nathan Road, though it does have a sign up in the road. Any resemblance between this gallery and its illustrious namesake off Piccadilly in London is, as they say, purely coincidental, but the shop is well worth the trouble of finding it.

At Sam's you can browse through a large book containing photographs of many of his famous clients; diplomats and politicians, as well as royalty – but you have to bend over the counter to do so to enable other customers to pass in the confined space. The shop is always full of British or American clients and the fitting room at the far end is little more than a cupboard accommodating one person at a time. Somehow people do manage to get in and out and enjoy a glass of beer which magically appears on the counter as soon as you enter. Sam makes beautiful suits and blouses for ladies as well as silk shirts, sports coats and suits for men.

An amusing anecdote was related in the British Press after Prime Minister Margaret Thatcher's visit to Hong Kong in 1982. She was accompanied by her husband, Denis, who went along to Sam and ordered some shirts. When they were finished he paid for them with travellers' cheques. Perhaps he was a little surprised on his return to England to get a letter from Sam saying that the bank had rejected one of the cheques as the signatures did not match. He immediately sent an apology and a personal cheque for the amount in question. Sam, never averse to publicity, did not cash it but put it in his window with the letter so that all may see the quality of his clientèle. Who could object to shirts at a discount in exchange for a boost in public relations?

Some of the glass doors and windows in the Nathan Road are so full of credit card signs that you cannot see in. Do not be fooled by this because, if you do produce one, the shopkeeper's pleasant smile may vanish and he is likely to point out that, as you are receiving such a bargain, you cannot expect him to be kept waiting for his money. If it involves a big sale the assistant may agree reluctantly or propose a 7 per cent card fee or perhaps you can split this down the middle? Alternatively you may find more accommodating salesmen else-where. Should you see a little red junk sign prominently displayed, this is the emblem of the Hong Kong Tourist Association. It means that the shopkeeper has been checked by the HKTA and agrees to abide by its ethical standards and adhere to fixed prices. Many crafts and jewellery shops have the same sign.

Jade is sold in shops everywhere but the famous Jade Market is something very special in Hong Kong. It spreads down one pavement of Canton Road practically sprawling into the street. Canton Road is a few hundred yards to the west of Nathan Road about one mile from the harbour. It is open daily from 10 o'clock in the morning until noon. It is always crowded with both local people and tourists, everyone seeking a bargain at one of the stalls. Who knows what you might find on one of the many makeshift tables, wrapped in yesterday's newspapers, or piled in assorted boxes. All manner of jade trinkets are displayed: goldfish, birds in flight, green-brown turtles, red-brown tigers, delicately-carved pastel butterflies, rings, bangles and strings of green beads, all at varying prices. It is whispered that exceptional jade ornaments do turn up every now and again at the Market. However, such instances are rare, and it is best to remember this. At midday, what had been a Jade Market becomes a Canton Road pavement again. Legends live on, however, and, while we in the West believe as children that there is a man in the moon, the Chinese children believe that there is a jade rabbit.

Walking north from Canton Road in the Yaumatei area you are alongside the large typhoon shelter where more boat people live. There seems to be everything available for them without ever needing to go ashore. They can send their children to floating schools, see a doctor, get a haircut, go to church, get supplies of fresh water and food and there is even the odd brothel and the notorious one-girl sampans. There is also the temple of the Tin Hau, protector of fisherfolk, which was originally near the water's edge and when land was reclaimed, was moved to Yaumatei.

Returning to Nathan Road, the southern section is known as the 'Golden Mile'. Not only is it lined with shops of all kinds, many tucked into galleries and alleys to increase the available frontage, but here also are two of the top class hotels, the Hyatt Regency and the Golden Mile Holiday Inn. The latter has 650 rooms and its dining and entertaining has a German atmosphere. There is the Baron's Table, a restaurant serving German provincial and continental food, the Baron's Tavern, a quiet bar for a drink before or after dinner and the Cafe Vienna, a Viennese-style Coffee House open every day from 6 a.m. to 2 a.m. The Golden Mile starts in the Tsimshatsui district close to the Star Ferry Terminal, an area where you will find Chinese opera and the traditional theatre shows. This is also the night life centre with many noisy discos, topless bars and in Hankow Road even one called 'Bottoms Up', for a change.

A recent visitor's survey show that the 'Golden Mile' and Tsimshatsui are the most popular shopping and entertainment centres, which explains the concentration of luxury hotels. Near to the New World Centre's large shopping complex stands the Regent on the very tip of Kowloon peninsula. It has some 600 rooms and of its restaurants 'Plume', with its enormous picture windows overlooking Victoria Harbour, offers a unique dining ambience. Unusually there are two levels connected by glass lifts. At night Plume's panorama is enthralling. Sparkling necklaces of lights outline the buildings up to the Peak itself. Neon signs pulsate in rainbow colours and spill out over the water silhouetting ships at anchor. But the view should not distract the gourmet for too long and he will return to the exquisite porcelain plates edged with golden plumes – inspired by the insignia of the Prince of Wales' feathers.

Plume's single sheet menu entices the epicure. While he ponders, a champagne-mix appears – champagne with a touch of blackberry juice – and further sleight of hand produces piping hot na'an bread, freshly baked in an authentic clay tandoori oven and accompanied by homemade goose liver pâté with green peppercorns. Plume's two Swiss chefs, Juerg Blaser and Silvio Blanchi, spend many months creating ideas and preparing dishes which are totally new and yet typical of Hong Kong.

Here is a delicious recipe called Grilled Seafood with a Dill Sauce.

Ingredients
6 scallops
1 pound lobster tail sliced into 6 medaillons
1 pound fresh garoupa sliced into 4 medaillons
6 large prawns
For the dill sauce:
6 large shallots
2 bunches of fresh dill
2 decilitres white wine
2 decilitres double cream
4 decilitres fish stock
salt and pepper
Garnish:
2 peeled tomatoes
1 bunch of dill

Method

Season the seafood and fish and grill all together. Simmer the white wine, shallots, dill and fish stock together reducing the quantity by 25 per cent. Add the double cream and reduce until smooth. Season with salt and pepper. Garnish the plates with sliced tomato and dill.

The opening of the Regent presented the usual problem to the management of how to create an event which would really attract attention. The Regent decided on 1000 bottles of Moet et Chandon, the Gurkha brigade pipe band, the Hong Kong Police orchestra and a Glenn Miller-style ensemble playing American musical selections.

Situated on the east Tsimshatsui waterfront the Shangri-La Hotel is only minutes from the airport. Walking through its inviting doors you find yourself in a truly spacious lobby which is over two storeys high and hung with glittering Viennese chandeliers. A large fountain is reflected in its gleaming marble floor. There is plenty of room for people to meet and, while waiting for friends, to enjoy two magnificent paintings by Malcolm Golding. As they measure 20 × 8 ft and 20 × 18 ft respectively, it required a considerable feat of engineering to move them when completed from the artist's temporary studio in the hotel, to their present position. The painting, entitled 'Shangri-La Valley', depicts Golding's own imaginary Shangri-La with a mystical red palace, and dark looming mountains and trees from which small animals peep out.

The Shangri-La Hotel is managed by Westin Hotels which is associated with United Airlines. It has 720 rooms and those on the twenty-first floor are run as an exclusive '21 Club' where a purser takes care of individual guest's needs.

Also adjacent to the business districts in Tsimshatsui east is a recent addition to Mandarin International Hotels, the Royal Garden. One of its unusual aspects is its construction on the atrium principle round a central court reaching 110 feet up to a vast skylight. It was necessary to enclose it because of the vagaries of the Hong Kong climate. The corridors leading to the rooms on each floor, 430 in all, form balconies overlooking the atrium and the floors in turn are reached by five glass lifts climbing up open tracks on the wall.

In the centre is an enchanting garden, an unbelievable oasis in the middle of bustling Kowloon, with trees, shrubs and flower beds. Knowing this, you will not be surprised when you book in at the reception desk to see what appears to be an outdoor scene within the building. An escalator takes you down to a lower level where there is yet another garden with a stream and a bridge across into a Chinese restaurant. However all the services of a modern deluxe hotel are here also including 3 restaurants, a health club, a business man's centre, a split level Victorian pub and conference facilities. All this within ten minutes of the airport and only a short walk from the cross-harbour tunnel and Mass Transit Railway.

Hong Kong has become such a holiday mecca that hotels seem to rise overnight. Space allows description of only a few but the reader will find a more complete list at the end of this book. Before leaving the subject I must mention one more in Kowloon, the Holiday Inn's 'Harbour View'. When the *Fung Shui* expert was consulted he was unhappy about the suggested colours of the menu covers which were duly changed to sky blue. However he was very enthusiastic about the logo of two golden carp, rather like the Pisces sign, except that the fish were back to back. It has certainly brought good fortune to the hotel. Such a sign was first used during the Sung Dynasty (AD 876), as a door symbol which brought blessing to those who passed in and out. It was used again during the Ming Dynasty (AD 1550) when government officials and nobles had jade buckles made in its form to enhance status. The name of the hotel 'Harbour View' speaks for itself as it offers a view of the constantly changing harbour scene. It is one of Holiday Inn's most luxurious hotels and each room has a full measure of all the facilities which the fastidious traveller has come to expect nowadays. Of course the bar is called 'The Golden Carp' and one of the most popular restaurants is 'The Mistral' which is Mediterranean both in decor and fare. Its specialities include pasta and pizzas.

Kai Tak airport, largely surrounded by part of the harbour, has some interesting places on its landward fringes. We failed to find the Sung Toi Rock which, according to legend, was carved as a memorial to Tai Ping. He was the last of the Sung emperors and he leapt into the water to escape the Manchus and was drowned in 1278. The Dragon Boat Festival is held each year to perpetuate his memory. However this legend seems to have become a trifle confused somewhere along the way. Yet another nobleman drowned himself in the fourth century and the festival claims to honour him also!

The airport itself is officially named Hong Kong International Airport but is always known as Kai Tak, the name of the people who used to own the land where the two-level terminal building now stands. Although virtually in the centre of Kowloon it is big enough for some 26 international airlines to use it and some four million passengers pass through it annually.

British Caledonian, British Airways and Cathay Pacific are the three carriers serving Hong Kong from the United Kingdom. British

Caledonian fly in seven days a week and added to airport facilities have opened a special city centre check-in service. In my experience, they certainly live up to their catch phrase: 'We never forget you have a choice.' British Airways have been flying between London and Hong Kong for 30 years and have a daily service. Cathay Pacific, was founded in 1946 by two enterprising wartime pilots and is still a private company owned by the Swire Group, serving most of the cities in the Far East.

Kai Tak amusement park with ferris wheels and stalls is close by as is Kowloon's City Market. There are many high and rather stark blocks of flats in the area and one, Li Chueng Uk, is called after a nobleman of that name whose tomb was unearthed during excavation work. His relics are now housed in a small museum in Tonkin Street which is open every afternoon except for Tuesday. Near the border to the New Territories, at Laichikok, is another amusement park complete with House of Horrors and roller skating rink, but the most important place to see there is Sung Dynasty Village. It is the perfect eye-opener for those who are really interested in the Chinese way of life and would like to know more about their customs.

Sung Dynasty Village is a personal dream come true for its owner and creator, Mr Deacon Chiu, who wished to revive interest in Chinese traditions and culture and to introduce a little Chinese history to visitors. Some of the village's 'props' (particularly in the House of Nobility) are from his personal antique collection. There are over 100 people who help and work in the village wearing authentic, traditional costumes.

For some two hours you can literally step into the past as you walk through the gate. You will be taken back 1000 years and amongst other things will receive some reproductions of Chinese money of the Sung period enclosed in a lucky red cover. The idea is that you can spend some of this at the various stalls you will visit and many people keep some of it as a souvenir. As you pause to make up your mind what to visit first you can watch a villager nearby who has some performing monkeys to amuse passers-by. Should you be interested in weapons there is a display in the village tower, immediately above the main entrance. Each item has been carefully made to scale, both in size and weight and, if you try to lift a spear, you will see just how strong warriors were in those days.

A river flows through the centre of the village crossed by several small bridges. In the old days river banks were often the centre for trade and a meeting place for inhabitants. There is a typical country market atmosphere here with hawkers selling toys and other oddments. Of course there is an eating house. It is the place where people linger because so much goes on there. It is an attractive two-storey building consisting of over 1000 carved wooden panels. It is called Plentiful Joy. You sit at small rosewood tables and the walls are hung with Sung paintings and calligraphy. You will be served authentic Sung food while being entertained by a magician or acrobat. Actually, at the time we were there, a cook, with even more sleight of hand than the magician, was making noodles with amazing dexterity. Beneath the restaurant lies Hong Kong's largest wax museum, containing effigies of emperors and other famous characters from the pages of China's 5000-year history.

The incense makers are interesting to watch in their workshop and there you can buy joss sticks to burn in the temple which is one of the most beautiful buildings. During the Sung Dynasty if a throw of bamboo sticks indicated bad luck, you could counteract this by entering the temple and beating the sacred drum three times. There is a statue of the god Erh Long in the temple accompanied by a replica of the heavenly hound, who is said to cause eclipses by attempting to swallow the sun and moon.

Delicious Sung pastries can be sampled in one of the pavilions, candy peanut brittle at another. A singer and two accompanying musicians perform in the village tavern where you can also sip a glass of wine. A special programme of entertainment is presented during each tour: demonstrations of kung fu, a traditional wedding ceremony, folk dances or acrobatics. You can watch the craftsmanship of the fan maker, have your fortune told or your name written in Chinese characters, or visit the Manor of Nobility, a rich man's house which has some very attractive rosewood furniture. The tea pavilion serves a special blend of green tea and has packets of it made up which you can buy. The souvenir shop sells many local items which have been manufactured exclusively for the Village. These include kimonos, porcelain, stationery, paper weights and wine. There are four daily group tours of the Village from Monday to Friday. The only drawback is that, once you are there, you hesitate to come back to the present-day world.

4 The New Territories and Outlying Islands

After compact Hong Kong, it often comes as a surprise that the New Territories cover an area of 370 square miles. North of the Kowloon peninsula this rural area was leased until 1997 from mainland China after Hong Kong had been colonised. So called because they were acceded well after Hong Kong Island and Kowloon, they contain settlements, ancient agricultural villages and, nowadays, thriving industries and modern towns. However most of the area serves as the bread basket for the colony and is given over to rice and vegetable growing and duck farming. Indeed, from the air, much of the landscape has a patchwork quilt appearance with its small squares of rice paddies and round ponds. Travel agencies run day tours or you can venture forth by rail or bus and you will find it a stimulating experience. Buses depart from the Jordan Road Ferry Bus Terminus in Kowloon. Trains to Sheung Shui, near the Chinese border, leave Hung Hom Railway Terminal in south-east Kowloon roughly every hour. You will find up to date information in the Hong Kong Tourist Association's *Places of Interest by Public Transport* leaflet.

Two interesting rock formations are pointed out on tourist visits to the New Territories, the first being Lion Rock which the winds have carved so realistically into a lion posed to spring that people often spot it before they are told. The other is called the Amah Rock on top of a hillock. It seems to depict an amah, or nurse, with a baby. She is said to be waiting for her fisherman husband who never came back, so a goddess turned her into stone.

Shatin is one of six new town developments designed to reduce the concentration of population in congested Hong Kong Island and Kowloon. Its many high-rise apartment blocks, factories, shops and offices are rapidly transforming what was once a quiet valley community into a major urban district. It has more to offer, however, than a reflection of Hong Kong's material needs. Under the wise guidance of a Norwegian missionary, an institution has been set up here which occupies a unique position in the Christian and Buddhist religions.

High on a hill, overlooking the changing landscape below, is the Christian mission of Tao Fong Shan – the Mountain of the Wind of Christ. Hidden from view, the only indication of its existence is a 40-foot (12 metres) cross standing above the treetops. The drive upwards to the monastery is beautiful. The road winds around in a series of Swiss-style hairpin bends through the wooded slopes and the brightly painted eight-sided building is sited at the top.

Today Tao Fong Shan is a study centre dedicated to ecumenical work and the role of the Christian Church among Chinese. Dr Karl Ludvig Reichelt set it up originally as a resting place for monks coming out of China, and now it continues on the ideals of the founder who discovered common ground between the teachings of Christianity and Buddhism. One of the original features of the centre has remained unchanged and is of considerable interest to tourists. A pottery was set up to enable wandering monks to work there and earn the means to continue as pilgrims. Nowadays some of the workers are handicapped people encouraged to become self supporting and a few were there in the time of the founder. Visitors can buy exquisitely decorated porcelain, some of which is exported.

There is yet another place of worship near Shatin, the famous Temple of 10,000 buddhas on the hillside above the railway station. You have to climb over 400 stone steps to reach it but it is well worth the effort. Statues of various gods guard it and in the main altar room you will see row upon row of tiny gilded buddhas whose benign expressions give an air of quietude and peace. In the temple grounds there is a nine-storey pagoda of Indian design, perpetuating the memory of Buddha believed to be one of the reincarnations of Vishnu. It is pink in colour and, if you have enough energy to climb to the top, there is a wonderful view.

Shatin is very proud of its university and modern campus, also its up-to-the-minute horse racing track built on reclaimed land like Happy Valley, but on a larger scale. To create the space for it, the tops of about a dozen hills were shaved off and the resulting spoil was used to fill in part of a nearby cove behind a retaining wall. The track is beautifully landscaped, the centre in particular having artificial ponds, flower beds and a Chinese gateway. Various types of grass were imported from different parts of the world to see which would withstand the Hong Kong climate and now there is a splendid green circuit. Just inside this an all-weather dirt course has been included

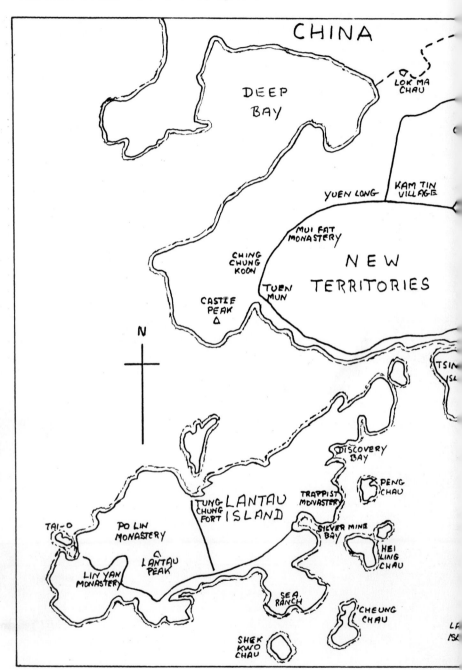

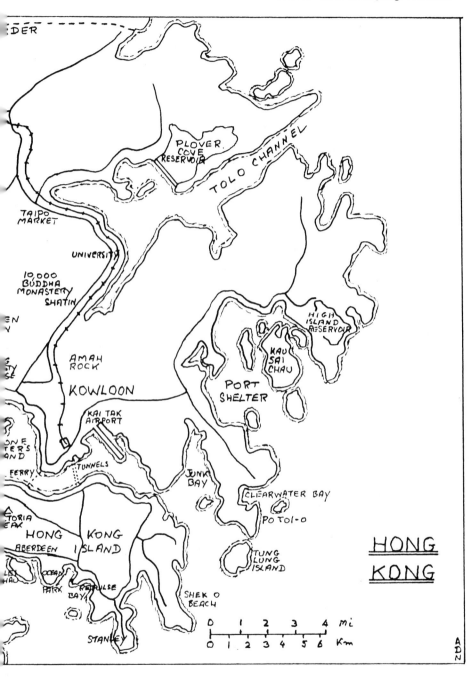

HONG KONG

12 The Toa Fung Shan Monastery at Shatin in the New Territories was set up in 1930 by a Norwegian Lutheran pastor as a resting place for Buddhists coming out of China, and now exists as a Christian mission.

which greatly increases its availability. Night meetings are held under floodlighting as at Happy Valley, and the Chinese love of gambling ensures the popularity of both courses. All the latest totalisator and computer betting facilities are installed, together with a vast matrix screen so that punters can literally ride alongside the horses.

Perhaps one of the most stimulating things about travel is that you get such contrasts in a short space of time. The name 'New Territories' brings a modern picture to mind which fits in with the racecourse. Yet when you leave it, within a short space of time you pass through countryside which has not changed for centuries. Buffalos patiently pulling aged ploughs, women gathering sugar cane or working on the roads, carrying the straw baskets with which they move the earth. Watching farm labourers setting rice one shoot at a time in the flooded paddies reminded me of the old Chinese fable of the Sung farmer. He wanted to grow rice more quickly and, as soon as the shoots appeared above the water, he spent much time pulling them upward and imagined he had enabled them to grow more quickly. He had of course destroyed the roots and instead of growing they had withered. The moral: you cannot fool nature.

Fishermen cast their nets in the same way as they have done for centuries, wearing the same costume. The uniform comprises black trousers and dark tunics for both sexes. The Hakka women still wear the type of hat that you have seen in children's books about old China – huge, round straw discs fringed with rouched black cloth to ward off the sun. Perhaps the only difference as far as the hats are concerned is that, in the old days the women would bow their heads so you could not photograph their faces. Nowadays they feel hurt if you do not use them as models. There are round holes in the crown of the hat because Hakka women wear a black cloth in bonnet fashion over their heads and this protrudes from the hole and again is a protection against the sun. The black curtain tends to create a cooling breeze about the head.

The quaint fishing village and town of Tai Po lies at the north-western corner of Tolo Harbour. From here you can take a ferry ride around the bay – that is if you can spare the time from Tai Po's market which has been famous for years, and once there it is difficult to leave. The name Tai Po means 'Buying Place'. Not only is there a large open market with stalls cheek by jowl, but along Fu Shing Street shop windows have displays which perhaps you can see more easily.

The market is unusual in that it has a mixture of every conceivable type of food, not only from the sea but also from the land. If you are fond of fish you will see all those you know and others you have heard

13 The grandstand at Shatin racecourse in the New Territories.

about but it is somewhat more difficult to recognise what comes from the farms. For instance, even if you enjoy Peking duck at the table, in the market you can buy just a quarter of a duck, but it is flattened to the shape of a pancake. The eggs might really be centuries old with their marbled brown and white stripes and those delicious sweet and sour pork pieces which you love in a Chinese restaurant rather resemble alabaster beads strung together. Fortunately things alive are easy to recognise – fat hens and chickens and lively fish in great vats. The exhilarating thing in a Chinese market is that everyone is having a good time and enjoying the bargaining.

While you are in this area you must visit the nearby Tai Ping Carpet Factory, a short distance from the town. Here you can see all the intricate phases of Chinese carpet manufacturing.

Between Tai Po and Plover's Cove is Bride's Pool, the only waterfall in the New Territories. A viewing site has been built for motorists overlooking it, and the fall makes up in beauty for being the only one. The story goes that a beautiful bride was on her way in a decorated rickshaw to her wedding when she asked to be shown the lovely view down into a valley. The rickshaw fell down the ravine, the bride vanished forever but at her demise a lovely crystal waterfall tumbled down the cliff face and has remained as a memorial ever since.

After that legend perhaps it is appropriate that the reservoir of Plover's Cove, a 40,000 million gallon water catchment, should be used as a youth centre. Picnic areas, caravan and camp sites have wooded enclosures and for the various youth movements which use it there is canoeing, fishing, swimming and all kinds of water sports.

Should you be motoring for the day in the New Territories perhaps the best place to stop for lunch would be the 'Better 'ole' bar and restaurant. Old soldiers would remember the famous First World War cartoon by Bruce Bairnsfather of his character Old Bill, sitting in a waterlogged shell hole with everything unpleasant flying overhead. Asked why he was sitting in such misery he replied: 'If you know a better 'ole go to it!' The luncheon we enjoyed there was not only delicious but had decorative flowers and leaves carved from vegetables in the centre of each plate. The restaurant has a charming oak-panelled bar and is near Fanling Station and the golf course of the same name. The Royal Hong Kong Golf Club has three eighteen-hole courses at Fanling. Visitors wishing to play should bring a letter of introduction from their hotel, travel agency or airline. At weekends you can play only if accompanied by a member.

At Lok Ma Chau there is a viewing platform on elevated ground, a vantage point from which you can look across the river into mainland China. Although there is a police post here it is not a recognised crossing point, but it does give an excellent panorama and many people, who actually do not wish to cross into China on a visit, come here to look and take photographs. There are the inevitable stalls with souvenirs, including the distinctive Hakka hats.

From Hong Kong you can easily take a day excursion to Canton. You will need a longer visit, which can also be arranged, if you wish to go further afield and each destination has its attractions. Peking has famous government buildings, the fantastic Forbidden City, Mao's elaborate crypt and the world's biggest square. Shanghai is more vital and more European. Hangchow is a tourist favourite because of its many gardens, parks, lakes and pagodas. Canton is a big old tropical city and very commercial. Probably the most requested city is Xian, in central China, where 2200 year-old, life-size, terracotta statues of a whole army are being unearthed.

However, to get back to the New Territories, there are also unusual places to see such as the curious walled villages. Perhaps the most interesting is Kat Hing Wai (sometimes referred to as Kam Tin) walled city, built during the 1600s, where all the people belong to the Tang clan. The town is encircled by a moat and has walls 18 feet (5 metres) thick and guard towers at each corner of its four sides; no wonder the 400 inhabitants have felt safe for centuries. There are even arrow slits and only one entrance gate, which has an interesting story attached to it. When the British took over Hong Kong the inhabitants resisted and, when it was captured, the gates were removed. Many years later their return was requested but for some time they could not be found. Eventually one of the pair was traced to Ireland and brought back. It was matched up locally and there they are to-day. They look impregnable and, as you walk in, you begin to wonder if you will ever get out again.

Then suddenly you are brought back to reality with requests for admission fees and even more money if you take photographs. A large central building is the Tang Ancestral Hall echoing today to the sounds of Kung Fu training, which is carried out in a side room off an inner courtyard. The hall is also a meeting place for village elders and a school for children. The history of the building is written on a stone tablet placed in the central room.

Near the new industrial city of Tuen Wan, Hong Kong's centre of the textile industry, is Castle Peak, used in olden times by the Imperial Coast Guard as a lookout post to protect the pearling fleets from pirates. Today there are two fascinating temples in the vicinity which are rewarding to visit. Widely believed to be one of the finest Buddhist temples in south-east Asia, Miu Fat is the newest one, having been finished only in 1980 at a cost of HK$60 million.

Built in traditional Chinese style Miu Fat has a most impressive entrance. On either side of a flight of eight wide stone steps sit gigantic white lions, with fierce expressions. They in turn are flanked by two white elephants which look very realistic, apart from their six tusks. As if these fearsome beasts were not enough to ward off evil spirits, two enormous red and gilded dragons twist and turn their way up the façade between open balconies. There are also a lot of mythical birds on the upturned double roofing.

The temple interior is resplendent with buddhas. In the main shrine hall there are three carved wooden statues covered in gold leaf. The central figure represents Sakyamuni, the founder of Buddhism; on his left the Lord of Western Paradise and on his right the Healing Buddha. Two things that charmed me in this temple more than anything else were the little lion at the bottom of the stair banister and the elegant sitting carved buddha on the wall facing him. The lion is small, benign and his head is smooth because of hands stroking him – and he loves it. The buddha is set in a moonlight scene and, by chance or design, sunlight from a side window illuminates him in shimmering light when the sun strikes through at mid afternoon.

The other temple is not far from Castle Peak hospital. It is the Ching Chung Koon and has a most beautiful garden. It is renowned for its bonsai trees. These dwarf trees are of every kind and most beautifully kept, some in flower beds, others in attractive pots or rounded troughs. Others again are lined along a low red brick wall. It is a strange experience to watch a breeze rustle such tiny leaves and cones, rather like looking through binoculars backwards. This Taoist temple is unusual in other ways also, for it acts as home for aged folk who have no means of support or relatives to look after them. It has a crematorium and the ashes of those cremated are stored in compartments in the walls for an annual rental with photographs or paintings of the departed. The money from this helps feed and house the inmates. There are many less macabre things which all can enjoy: intricately designed lanterns centuries old, a library of several thousand books, parchments which tell the history of Taoist religion and a precious jade seal more than 1000 years old. The main hall has green and red rafters. The roof is joined to the building by carved wooden lattice work in gold and red. The temple is dedicated to one of the Taoist immortals, Lui Tung Bun. Born in AD 789, he was a missionary inspired by a dream. Taoist mythology states that he had

14 Miu Fat Monastery in the New Territories at Castle Peak is widely believed to be one of the finest Buddhist temples in south-east Asia. Completed in 1980 it cost HK$60 million and contains over 10,000 sculptures and paintings of Buddha.

15 A worship hall at the Ching Chung Koon Taoist Monastery in the Tuen Mun area of the rural New Territories. The Monastery is noted for its well-kept gardens and collection of bonsai plants.

wondrous powers, a sword for slaying devils and magic fly switch which is displayed by his statue.

As you wander around the gardens and pavilions you will see several ponds. The one containing turtles is supposed to bring good luck if you are fortunate enough to toss in a coin and have it bounce off a turtle's head. Should you feel peckish there are food stalls where you can purchase tasty vegetable snacks. While visiting the temple grounds one day we happened to arrive in the midst of a flower show.

Hong Kong has quite a long traditon of forestry, with trees being planted in water-catchment areas to prevent soil erosion. Many were cut down during the Japanese Occupation in the last war but have been replaced. In fact, although Hong Kong has an image as a place of high-rise skyscrapers and crowded streets, 40 per cent of its land area is set aside for country parks and three areas in the rural New Territories were among the first to be designated as such. These are named after well-known features: Shing Mun, Kam Shan (or Golden Hill) and Lion Rock. Others have been added more recently and there are now 21 and two 'special areas'. There are some villages in the parks, as the intention is not to create museums, but to allow normal life to continue in harmony with the countryside. A small team in each one has the job of looking after the trees, maintaining paths and facilities, collecting litter, prevention and fighting of fire – all the one-hundred-and-one jobs needed to protect the land at the same time as helping public enjoyment of it. Large scale maps have been drawn by the Crown Lands and Survey Office and nature trails, a long distance hiking trail and activities for children have been developed. Barbecuing is allowed at about 3000 sites situated in safe spots throughout the areas. Anyone found lighting a fire elsewhere than a proper barbecue place is liable to a stiff fine.

These country parks provide a home for a wide variety of the indigenous animal population of Hong Kong, including leopard cats, fruit bats, turtles, cobras, tree frogs, foxes and badgers. The days are long past when elephants and tigers roamed South China but it was only in 1915 that the last tiger was shot in Hong Kong – after devouring two unlucky police officers. Its head is still on display at the Central Police Station. A Protection Ordinance was passed in 1981 to protect all local birds and mammals to discourage commercial dealings.

A set of Hong Kong stamps issued in May 1982 featured four of the rarer local wild animals: the five-banded civet, the pangolin, the porcupine and the muntjac, or barking deer. The first three are nocturnal with solitary habits and are difficult to see but you may be lucky enough, if on a daytime hill walk, to catch a glimpse of the barking deer although he is very timid. But even if you do not get an actual sighting of him he can be heard at night during the mating season when the sound he makes is like a raucous dog bark. The five banded civet has five broad black and white bands on his tail and at the throat. You might at night hear a porcupine for if he is irritated he will make a rattling sound with his hollow quills.

The pangolin can be 2 to 3 feet (60 to 90 cms) in length and weigh up to 12 lbs (5 kg). It climbs trees and can dig holes with large, long claws on its fore and hind feet. It has no teeth but can lick up termites, ants and wasps vigorously with its long, sticky tongue. In the past gourmets valued the pangolin, which is now a protected species, believing that its scales possessed the aphrodisiacal properties proclaimed by traditional Chinese literature.

One of the interesting projects in the New Territories is the Kadoorie Experimental Farm two or three miles West of Taipo. There is a story behind the birth of the idea. The father of the present Kadoorie brothers, Lord Laurence Kadoorie of Kowloon and Horace Kadoorie, walked from Baghdad to Shanghai years ago, a Jewish wanderer. There he built up a vast fortune including considerable financial interests in Hong Kong, though never able to read or write. When the communists took over in China he was expropriated and moved to Hong Kong where he again expanded his empire. Not being a man to bear a grudge, when refugees from China started flooding into Hong Kong, he proposed to the Government that the farmers among them be allocated a parcel of land and money to get them restarted. The Kadoories would provide them with a house, seeds and livestock. The money was not to be a gift but a repayable loan over a period of time thereby turning them into mini-capitalists. The idea was adopted and has proved enormously successful turning the New Territories into a bread basket for Hong Kong. To provide the seed and livestock the Experimental Farm was set up and it now has many notable achievements to its credit. For instance the communists had slaughtered all the white Peking ducks but, starting with 14 fertile eggs, the Farm created the present supply. The typical Chinese pig was a scrawny, sway-backed animal although pork is a mainstay of the Chinese diet. By selective cross-breeding the Farm has stocked the New Territories with splendid, straight-backed porkers which produce the right balance of meat. To-day, among his other interests, Lord Kadoorie controls Hong Kong Light and Power which is building an atomic power station, part of whose output will be fed to China.

The New Territories and Outlying Islands

Driving back from the New Territories into Kowloon one is struck by the contrast between the spacious, old-fashioned countryside and the crowded modern metropolis. Yet each gives mutual support to the other. The Territories provide much of the urban food requirements and recreational facilities and the third largest banking centre in the world makes development capital available and provides the market. It is able to do this because its industries have enormous export capacity. So what is to happen in 1997 when the lease expires on the New Territories? If China takes them back Hong Kong and Kowloon could not stand on their own as a viable unit. The Chinese say they want to regain sovereignty but not destroy prosperity. Almost certainly the two are indivisible. It is thrusting enterprises which have produced the phenomenon you see today. Perhaps the best answer for the moment is to remember the old Chinese toast, 'May you live in interesting times.'

First-time visitors to Hong Kong are often surprised to find that Hong Kong itself is only one of 236 islands on the east side of the Pearl River estuary, although many of these are uninhabited. Nevertheless, the Outlying Districts Ferry Pier in Hong Kong is busy all day handling the traffic to and from Silvermine Bay and Tai O on Lantau, Cheung Chau Island, Peng Chau Island and Lamma Island. Triple-decker air-conditioned ferries leave at regular intervals. Each of these islands, in additon to many others which are not served by public ferries, has its own individual character and charm. Lantau is the largest, indeed it is nearly twice the size of Hong Kong island, though with a sparse population of some 20,000 at present. Naturally, in the thrusting commercial atmosphere of the territory, there are plans for development, and it may prove to be the site of Hong Kong's new airport.

Most of Lantau's inhabitants at present live in and around Tai O, an attractive old fishing port whose main street has a stream running down the centre. It has been said that the day's catch and the day's wash hang on the same bamboo poles and lines to dry. Not surprising, when many of the houses are built on stilts above the water. Silvermine Bay is a resort and is crowded at weekends. It has a fine beach with paved pathways for cyclists. A bus service from here can take you to visit Po Lin (Golden Lotus) monastery on one of the highest points on the island. A series of hairpin bends takes you up some 2400 feet (730 metres) to the buddhist monastery from which you can enjoy a magnificent view of the island. The temple is a large, ornate one with several pavilions. You can spend the night here and enjoy their simple food. Many visitors rise before dawn and go with a guide up Lantau Park to watch the sunrise. Close to this temple there is a tea plantation of some 60 acres (24 hectares). If you visit it you will be tempted to taste the tea and, if you enjoy it, perhaps buy a packet or two to take home and bring back memories.

At Tung Chung, on the northern side of the island, the ramparts of an old fort dating back to 1817 are still standing. Six cannon point seawards as if still warding off the attacks of former pirates. The Trappist monastery of Our Lady of Joy is on another hillside overlooking the east coast. A most interesting place, it has to be reached in three stages. You take the ferry from Hong Kong to Peng Chau (a small island off Lantau) then the monastery's own shuttle ferry across to Lantau, where from the landing stage it is an uphill walk of about quarter of an hour. Again it is a place where you can spend the night or just have a simple vegetarian meal. During the Chinese Civil War the monks fled from Peking and have been on Lantau ever since. The monastery was completed in 1956.

The tiny island of Peng Chau has several cottage industries such as metalwork, woodwork and porcelain and most ferries stop there going to and from Lantau.

Several new recreational developments are coming to fruition on Lantau. The major one, at Discovery Bay, covers an area of 1500 acres and will take some time to complete. Current plans include development of the beach area, construction of an hotel, holiday flats, a shopping centre, playgrounds, parks and eventually, two international-standard golf courses. I have seen the plans and they are very exciting. They will include a direct ferry service from Central covering the 10-mile (15-kilometre) journey in 25 minutes and it looks as if the beautifully sited bay will become a complete town in its own right in due course.

The HK$50 million Sea Ranch development, on the southernmost tip of the Chi Ma Wan Peninsula, is now nearing completion and consists of 14 four-storey chalets containing 152 apartments set in landscaped gardens with a two-storey club house. Recently, plans for the Lantau Country Club, adjoining the Sea Ranch site, have been revived. It will comprise an hotel with restaurant facilities, some 300 condominium apartments and a wide range of recreational facilities. Other hotel and resort projects on a smaller scale are also in the pipeline.

Cheung Chau, ('chau' means 'island'), always described as 'dumb-bell shaped', is where the annual 'Bun' festival takes place to which you find a reference in Chapter 1. A favourite lair of pirates at one time, it is a peaceful place today without even a car to avoid when crossing a street. There is no pollution of any kind on this island, unless you dislike the pungent smell of drying fish. The harbour is crammed with fishing boats of all kinds and you can watch how they are built by walking along the waterfront. There is a Taoist temple, Pak Tai, dedicated to a saint who is accredited with dispersing a plague. It is only a short distance from the ferry landing. There are good beaches, fresh seafood and a restful atmosphere – except during the 'Bun' festival when the island is crowded with merrymakers.

The island of Lamma, is the third largest of Hong Kong's many islands. About 6000 people live in its two small towns and some coastal villages. Many of these are commuters from Hong Kong and Kowloon. It is less than 2 miles (3 km) south of Aberdeen, yet it remains an island of green slopes, pretty bays and fishing villages. A favourite place for weekend boat trippers and yachting parties, it is best visited during weekdays when it is quiet. It is useful to remember that ferry fares double on Sundays and public holidays, and sometimes after 12.30 p.m. on Saturdays.

Apleichau Island is only a short distance from Aberdeen across a bridge, and has one of the largest boat building yards in Hong Kong. All types are made here including speed boats, cruisers, sloops, ferry boats, yachts and lighters as well as sampans and junks. If this sort of thing appeals to you it is well worth a visit and you may be lucky enough to meet somebody who speaks some English who can take you round. Junks and sampans need no blueprints and are created by eye from long years of experience.

1 Hong Kong Island from Kowloon.

2 View of Victoria Harbour by night.

3 Hung Hom terminus of the Kowloon-Canton railway.

4 Victoria Harbour and waterfront from Causeway Bay.

5 Chinese Food and Drink

A few years ago The Mandarin Hotel gave an imperial banquet for a couple of dozen gourmets which was said to have cost some US$20,000 and lasted the traditional three days. Among the exotic foods ordered from abroad were honey-heart abalone from Japan, spotted deer from Africa, the best shark's fin from the Indian Ocean, and birds' nests from Thailand. To mention a few unusual delicacies, the menus boasted crane's legs, bear's paws and civet cat. From China came 2400 rice birds for their succulent tongues and from France frogs' legs were each boned and stuffed with mushrooms and a bamboo shoot. In dynastic days such resplendent feasts were interspersed with music, discussions, drinking, tasting tit bits, erotic pastimes and much laughter and joking. The Mandarin's deliciously cooked foods, wines and the sheer luxury of it all caused a ten-minute ovation for the head chef at the last repast who, it is said, after his exit collapsed for 18 hours!

Chinese cuisine has become popular over the last decade everywhere and the homes of many of the best Chinese chefs now wielding their 'woks' (the traditional, rounded-base Chinese frying pans) are in London, New York, Paris and other faraway cities. Whether a feast be a banquet for the wealthy or a birthday party for those with little money, all Chinese believe that every glass of wine and every slice of meat is pre-ordained, so each must be presented in perfect condition and exquisitely arranged on the table.

If things go wrong in any way for family or friends the Chinese will do their best to give aid and, although it may be nothing to do with food, it is called 'sharing the rice bowl'. Food, of course, is the mainstay of life, but the Chinese never forget that it is. The good life is said to consist of three essentials: live in Soochow, a city noted for its refined manner and beautiful women; eat in Kwangchow (Canton); and be buried in Liuchow where teak wood coffins are made.

16 Expert chef, Mr Choy Cheuk demonstrates to his students his mastery with the Chinese wok.

Average Hong Kong families do not have much money but spend a great deal of it on their meals because, like the French, they adore food and spend a lot of time preparing it. As the French buy bread twice a day so the Hong Kong housewife shops twice a day so that each fish, fruit or vegetable is absolutely fresh for the next meal. There is a saying that cooking is, 'an ancient art of ultimate harmony – pleasing to the eye, mouth-watering, a delight to the palate.'

If the visitor is trying Chinese food for the first time he cannot do better than start with *dim sum*. The Cantonese are renowned for making dozens of these different specialities and there are *dim sum* restaurants everywhere. Unlike the French this time the Chinese love food in little snacks throughout the day. Tiny pastries and dumplings can be savoury or sweet, the difficulty is to know what the pastry encloses. The Hong Kong Tourist Association has a leaflet which explains the mysteries with small drawings, and explanations of what each is in Chinese and English. You may be able to ask for them by name but by far the easiest thing to do if the waiter looks puzzled is to point to the pictures. The savoury *dim sum* are either deep fried or steamed. The former are crispy and contain such ingredients as bean roll filled with pork, shrimp and oyster sauce, or rice flour triangle filled with pork, shrimp and bamboo shoots, or fried roll filled with shredded pork, chicken, mushrooms, bamboo shoots and bean sprouts.

Of the steamed *dim sum* there are dumplings with minced pork and shrimp, stuffed with shrimps alone, assorted meats or tiny pieces of spare ribs with red pepper sauce. It is always satisfying to end with a sweet *dim sum* such as a crisp sweet cake topped with almonds or coconut or even have a small coconut 'snowball'. *Dim sum* is served throughout the day until about 5 o'clock in the afternoon. Choosing is easy because not only can you have a leaflet but you can peep into the little bamboo baskets the waitresses push around on trolleys. Before you pay your bill the waitress will count up your little dishes or baskets and tell you what you owe. You can have endless tea and if you leave the lid off your pot it is taken as a sign that you would like it refilled. The name *dim sum* means 'Heart's Desire'. New *dim sum* are being invented all the time and you are not expected to eat more than one or two if you are not feeling very hungry. If you order three or four of the steamed variety they are served in small containers one on top of the other to keep them hot. The top one will have a round lid and the bottom of the little shallow basket fits into the next one.

If you think you might like to try a breakfast of *dim sum* and tea, as many Chinese do perhaps after an early morning walk, you can be served in several 'early morning' restaurants. On Hong Kong Island there is the Luk Kwok Hotel at 67 Gloucester Road in Wanchai, the Dim Sum Kitchen in Food Street and the Pearl City Restaurant at 22 Paterson Street, the two latter in Causeway Bay. At 24 Stanley Street in Central the Luk Yu Teahouse is another pleasant place for a *dim sum* breakfast. The doors open at 7.30 a.m. and as you wait for your order look around at the period decor as it has been open for over 40 years. Ceiling fans whirl and the walls are covered in framed scrolls and antique mirrors. It is named after a connoisseur of tea who lived during the Tang Dynasty. Some of the teas you may drink here have been left to ferment for years to improve their flavour. 'Heung Peen' (fragrant leaf) green and 'Bo Lei' black teas both go well with *dim sum* and are usually available.

Known for its colour, fragrance and taste, Cantonese food specialises in retaining natural flavour, particularly in the preparation of seafood. Mr. Choy, a famous chef, says that timing is a vital consideration. His method of achieving the correct cooking time is interesting. The fish is taken from the wok when it is about 80 per cent cooked and placed in its piping hot dish. It is covered and the remaining 20 per cent cooking takes place while it is on the way to the table. When the waiter removes the cover the fish is succulent, tender and perfectly cooked.

The *chef de cuisine* in a Chinese kitchen is the stir-fry cook. The oil is always well above boiling point and his timing must be perfect. His main tools are the wok and the chopper, a razor sharp knife with a blade about eight inches long and three inches wide which serves as slicer, chopper, spatula, strainer and general kitchen weapon and is seldom out of his hand. He decides on sauces and flavourings and lifts the result out deftly with chopsticks.

Some of the strange sounding dishes beloved by the Cantonese are ancient eggs, chickens feet, fish lips, and three very expensive soups made of birds' nests, shark's fin and snakes. The bird's nest is only one of several ingredients in the soup of that name, but it is the one which provides the exotic flavour. It is expensive because the nests are difficult to get, being built in high, almost inaccessible cliffs above the sea. The part of the nest used is the solidified saliva of the bird with which it 'knits' the nest together. Snake soup is only found on winter menus because the meat is considered good to keep you warm in cold weather. To add a touch of glamour it is served sprinkled with lemon grass, and chrysanthemum blossoms. The snakes come from China duty free!

It is part of folklore that the Chinese prize eggs which have been buried for a century or more and then dug up from the ground as carefully as if excavating ancient Roman mosaics; the taste is supposed to be ambrosial. In contrast to Westerners who like fresh hen eggs in their dishes, the Chinese show preference for preserved, salted duck eggs which go through various stages of artificial ageing such as being left in lime for a few weeks. These are sold wrapped in straw and both the yolk and white are black. They are usually served raw and the Chinese eat them with ginger. Salted duck eggs have a black outer layer and, when cooked, the inside looks exactly like a hard boiled egg, except that it is salty. The black outer layer is scraped off and the egg cleaned thoroughly before cooking with rice.

Chicken feet have long been a delicacy. One of the nicest *dim sum* is chicken feet in black bean sauce. When you think we consider calves' foot jelly a delicacy it is not dissimilar, but very laborious to prepare. The claws have to be removed and also the skin after boiling so it takes quite a large quantity to yield a worthwhile amount of jelly.

I was told a story about chicken feet which is perhaps apocryphal. One of Hong Kong's enterprising businessmen was being shown over a modern chicken processing plant in the U.S.A. He was most impressed with the way in which the birds were plucked, gutted, sectioned and frozen, but his frugal mind was troubled that the feet were thrown away as waste. He asked if he could have a container load of them delivered to Hong Kong and this was arranged. When they arrived in perfect condition however the container was marked 'unfit for human consumption' in accordance with American food regulations. He managed to circumnavigate this hazard and sold them profitably, but requested that future containers should not have this marking. The next one arrived marked 'unfit for human consumption except in Hong Kong'.

A great winter delicacy to keep out the cold is snake meat added to various dishes. Indeed no part of the reptile is wasted: the meat is delicious; the venom is exported for use as serum; even the gall bladder is considered a cure for rheumatism. To quote an old Chinese saying 'While the autumn winds are blowing high, the five snakes are getting fat'. The snakes referred to are the cobra, the Asiatic rat snake, the banded krait, the copper race and the hundred flower; these are deemed the finest for cooking. Snake dishes are prepared in a variety of ways and among them, snake broth is hightly rated by gourmets. The soup is made from three to five different types of snake meat, shredded chicken and other ingredients including fish stomachs, ham, water chestnuts, bamboo shoots and mushrooms. Chrysanthemum petals, lemon leaves and crisps are popularly added when it is served. Chinese medieval theories claim that snakes can strengthen the brain, the waist and the legs, enhance physical vigour and keep the body warm in cold temperatures.

The majority of restaurants in Hong Kong are Cantonese but there are also many Pekingese ones. Peking food, coming from colder northern China, is more substantial. Instead of the traditional rice, wheat takes over and more bread and noodles are used, with deep as well as stir frying. Fresh water fish like carp are favourites as are lamb, poultry and especially duck.

Who has not heard of Peking duck? I have watched one being prepared but it is most difficult to do and I have not attempted it. The wing tips are removed and an incision made where the wing meets the breast into which a length of rubber tube is inserted between the skin and the flesh. You hold the bird and air blown in, until the whole duck is inflated and the skin separated from the meat. Next ginger is added to boiling water and the duck is scalded until the skin is white. Then the neck aperture is tied up with string and hung in an airy place for about four hours to dry and allow the skin to harden. Syrup added to boiling water is then poured over the bird and again it is suspended from a hook and allowed to air dry for a further hour.

Finally it is roasted for another hour and a half, meanwhile being basted with sesame oil at 15-minute intervals, before serving. No wonder it is so delicious. My recipe adds that, if the duck is for later use, deep fry in peanut oil and a soup can be made from the bones. The skin of the duck is the most prized part, served sizzling hot. Pieces are spread with a little plum jam and a spring onion placed on top. The whole is wrapped in a thin pancake and eaten with the fingers.

Beggar's Chicken is another popular Peking dish. The name does not suit it for it is fit for a prince. The stuffing is a mixture of vegetables including mushrooms and onions. The bird is then wrapped in lotus leaves, sealed in clay and baked. It arrives for you to admire in its ash-blackened state (perhaps the reason for the name) and when this is cracked it is so tender that it is claimed you could cut it with chopsticks.

If you like Swiss fondue you will enjoy cooking a Mongolian barbecue, which is similar to those served in Taiwan, at your table. You choose raw ingredients from bowls of various foods laid out on a side board. Back at your own table you dip what you have chosen into marinating dishes and then cook your tit-bits on an oiled hotplate.

Hot pot dishes and spicy sauces are not the monopoly of Pekingese cooking for the Hakka farmers in the New Territories have their own versions. Their salted chicken is well known, as is their stuffed duck.

The latter has bones removed through a hole in the neck and is then stuffed with rice, chopped meats and lotus seeds. The Hakka people are said to prepare the best tasting curd, a type of white custard made from the soya bean which is the basis for many vegetarian concoctions.

The names of many dishes even when written in English do not convey much to visitors, but waiters are only too willing to explain.

Phoenix chicken is breast of chicken stir-fried in seasoned oil. The meat is then sliced and served with preserved ham and peas, surrounded with a garnish of cabbage, carrots, mushrooms, water chestnuts and bamboo shoots.

Shrimp toast is mouth-watering. Squares of bread are lightly toasted then combined with pre-marinated shrimps. Dipped in egg and flour batter, the shrimps and toast are stir-fried quickly, then served garnished with cabbage and parsley.

Winter melon pond is a delicious type of thick soup made of delicately flavoured chicken stock served in a hollowed out and carved winter melon. Added to this are diced mushrooms, lobster, chicken, ginkgo nuts, abalone, peas, preserved ham, bamboo shoots and water chestnuts – a whole meal in a melon.

Fortunately many names mean just what you read such as:

Sweet and sour pork, the well known sweet and sour taste in a dish of pork chunks, green peppers and carrots.

Sweet and sour whole fish, a special fish found only in the South China Sea, deep-fried then served with sweet and sour sauce.

Fried pork slices, thin strips of pork dipped in egg white and corn flour, boiled in a mixture of red peppers, soy sauce, ginger and water and then stir fried.

Red hot pepper chicken, diced chicken dipped in egg white and corn flour then stir fried along with red peppers, peanuts, vinegar and soy sauce.

Chinese food differs from European in two ways. It is devoid of dairy products and there are no desserts of the kind we have in the West. Fresh fruit often ends a meal and Chinese adore fruit of all kinds. As a proof of this, fruit shops and stalls seem to be working 24 hours a day.

Toffee Apples are one of the favourites to end a lavish meal. The fruit is peeled, dipped into toffee syrup, deep fried and then quickly plunged into cold water so that the toffee hardens and encases the apple. Sometimes slices of banana are added. Salads are made with all kinds of fresh fruit but the best loved of all ingredients remains the lychee – most prized of all oriental fruits. Lychees grow in Taiwan and are shipped abroad in tins of sugar syrup. Should you enjoy them you will find an easy way to make a sorbet for there is a recipe on some tins suggesting that, as the syrup takes on the flavour of the lychees, if you add a tablespoon of fresh lemon juice to it, partially freeze it then fold in a whipped egg white, you need only freeze the result until it is firm. A tale is told of the Empress Yang Kwei-Fei who squandered her husband the Emperor's fortune on horsemen to ride the 2000 miles constantly across the provinces to keep up a supply of lychees for the royal table.

When visiting temples it is interesting to note the lovely arrangements of fresh fruits displayed on white porcelain plates at the Buddha's feet. It is an art akin to flower arranging. Like vegetable carving, even the dried fruits in jars look attractive, but then so are the jars. Ginger jars are as elaborate as tea caddies and have always been collectors' pieces. Gifts in the form of Chinese jars containing ginger in a sugar solution used to be sent back to Britain as Christmas presents in early Hong Kong days. The Chinese use ginger fresh, chopped or sliced in small pieces, to add flavour to various foods or to act as a digestive aid. A further digestive aid used at one time in the North where the food is heavier was to serve sweets between courses on little plates. These were usually doughy creations often in the shape of birds or animals. The idea was to cleanse the palate, and prepare the way for an entirely new taste with the next round of dishes, rather as we use bread between courses for the same purpose.

A great favourite, used as a sort of petit fours is a dried date, split and rolled around a walnut or peanut. Fruits preserved in sugar are also popular such as apples, pears, apricots, peaches and, that most delightful of all, Chinese plums. These are usually packed in glass jars in a sugary mixture. Black plums, known as *mei*, have a sweet-sour taste. Before being placed in the sugar solution they are dried but retain a sharp flavour. More pleasant to our taste is another plum called *yangmei* which is virtually unknown except to the Chinese and has the extraordinary quality of tasting exactly like a fresh strawberry.

You will often see children eating something out of little cardboard cylinders. This is *shan cha*, another kind of plum which is pressed with sugar and made into a red powder which again has a sweet-sour taste. Sometimes it is consolidated into a block and it is believed also to have a therapeutic value. It is supposed to reduce blood pressure and make one slim and is offered by herbalists to sweeten the mouth after a draught of particularly unpleasant medicine.

The setting of a Chinese table is elegant but simple. From the left there is a bowl and spoon, a plate for left-overs, a small divided dish with perhaps chilli sauce and mustard, a dish of soy sauce, silver serving spoon and chopsticks. If you hold the china spoon up to the light you will notice that the bowl part looks as if a few grains of rice are embedded in it. This is traditional. The rice dries up in the firing and leaves the shape of the grains in the porcelain.

Once you learn how to use chopsticks you wonder why you ever found it difficult but it takes a little time before you become adept. You take them in your hand so that the ends are level, one above the other. Both are held by the thumb against the side of the index finger, spaced about one inch apart, and this acts as a hinge. The bottom one is held steady by the third and fourth fingers while the first and second move the top stick. Observation of Chinese at the table will also disclose that it is quite polite to raise the bowl to chin level and 'shovel' the more slippery morsels into the mouth with the sticks. Soup, of course, is either drunk from the bowl or with the china spoon.

'A learned guest is the main delicacy of the feast,' states a Chinese proverb. Also the Chinese delight in showing hospitality to strangers

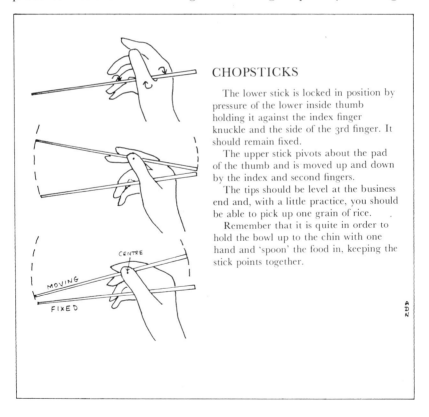

CHOPSTICKS

The lower stick is locked in position by pressure of the lower inside thumb holding it against the index finger knuckle and the side of the 3rd finger. It should remain fixed.

The upper stick pivots about the pad of the thumb and is moved up and down by the index and second fingers.

The tips should be level at the business end and, with a little practice, you should be able to pick up one grain of rice.

Remember that it is quite in order to hold the bowl up to the chin with one hand and 'spoon' the food in, keeping the stick points together.

as well as friends and sharing their cooking skills. The Hong Kong Tourist Association has arranged several cooking courses for visitors varying in duration. A day course can either be a demonstration followed by the cooking of three dishes or watching some six dishes being cooked. The most popular course for tourists is the three-day one. This consists of demonstrations, sampling different types of food in various restaurants, and visiting local food markets. If you take a week's course it includes cooking *dim sum* and all kinds of Chinese dishes, including roasts, and vegetable carving. The latter is considered of exceptional importance and some of the work is so artistic it is difficult to believe such lovely designs can be made from food.

'Courtesy pleases much and costs little' claims a Chinese proverb but customs differ very much from ours, especially when entertaining guests. The Chinese always exchange toasts when raising their wine cups at formal lunch or dinner parties. It is considered courteous to hold the cup with one hand and touch the base with the other. The host usually begins the meal by toasting his guests. '*Kan pei*' (pronounced 'gam bay', meaning 'dry cup') is the equivalent of 'Bottoms up!' If in offering a toast you do not want to *Kan pei*, just say '*Suei yi*' ('As you please'). This means you give the person you toast and yourself the option of drinking all or part of the contents of the cup.

Do not be surprised if, at a formal lunch or dinner, you are seated opposite your host instead of next to him. This means that you are the guest of honour. The host always sits with his back to the door, and the guest of honour facing it. Tea served at the end of a meal means the party is over and it is time to go, even if your host, out of politeness, suggests that you stay longer.

There is no agreement among scholars about the first mention of tea. Certainly it seems the Chinese were the first to discover its merit and likened it to 'Heaven's sweetest dew'. It also seems that Emperor Chinnung (2737 BC), who is credited with the beginnings of all medical and agricultural knowledge, knew of its existence. Legend has it that it was introduced to China by an Indian ascetic, Bodhidharma, who came to China on a missionary expedition in AD 543 and yet tea was mentioned in the poetry of Confucius before that date. After that, all is conjecture until AD 780 when Yo Lu of the Tang Dynasty wrote a narrative on the growing, picking, gathering, processing and drinking of the delicious herb.

Although Marco Polo was received by the great Mongol, Kubla Khan, in AD 1275 and appointed to a governorship, strangely he makes no mention of tea in his writings. The Portuguese, ahead in most Far Eastern commodities in Europe, did little to extol it and it took the Dutch to sing its praises first and then the British who became besotted with it and to this day cannot do without it.

The much quoted passage from Samuel Pepys's diary written on 25th September, 1660 states, 'I did send for a cup of tea, a China drink, of which I had never drunk before' which proves what a novelty tea was at that time. The East India Company presented the King with a gift of one pound and two ounces, and two years later with another parcel containing 22 pounds, costing the directors 50 shillings a pound. It remained a special drink for royalty and grandees for some time due to its expense.

The Chinese have always felt that tea was a sacred part of life and the making and drinking of it an art to be cultivated just as the Japanese have their tea ceremony. It is not only today that water is believed to make such a difference to the taste. It has been a fact since tea was first gathered. An eighteenth-dynasty emperor, Ching Lung, not only demanded certain tea leaves but insisted that each type had to have its own special water. His favourite water he called the 'lightest'. His joy was great when it was discovered that the source of the best water for a certain type of tea was close to the tea garden where the leaves grew. He stationed a company of his soldiers around the area to prevent damage and theft. While travelling around his domain he inspected and listed the many fountains according to their water. The 'lightest' of waters were always considered the best, and his favourite was the Jade Fountain on the outskirts of Peking.

The earliest type of tea caddies that came to Europe and America were like the well-known ginger jars in blue and white porcelain. The word caddy is a corruption of the Chinese word 'catty', a measure of weight slightly more than one pound which was usually the amount of tea in it. Caddies have gone through all shapes and sizes and been both expensive and inexpensive. In early days they became more and more elaborate and were made in lovely designs of pewter, tortoise-shell, inlaid wood, brass and silver. Each had a lock and key. During tea parties the hostess would make and pour the tea herself after first unlocking the caddy and blending the tea leaves from little drawers. Leaves varied in colour from black to pale green. Today these caddies are collectors' pieces.

Teas are just as carefully blended today as they have always been and each person has his or her favourite. There is Chinese tea noted for its delicate taste, jasmin blossom best drunk unadulterated, and lemon-scented which is delicious hot or iced. Tea served at breakfast, usually with the addition of milk and sugar is very popular; one famous breakfast tea, Lady Londonderry, is a blend of Ceylon, Indian and Taiwanese leaves originally blended for one of London's most famous social and political hostesses of the first half of this century. Perhaps part of the popularity of tea is its consistency for some and its endless variety for others.

Tea stories are many and I have witnessed two which caused much merriment. At a party attended by a distinguished Indian guest the hostess was pouring tea. 'How do you like our English custom of tea drinking?' she enquired. 'Very much indeed', came the reply, 'you see I was born in Assam which produced it.' On another occasion I was with a party of tourists in Egypt visiting Sakkara on a hot afternoon. Suddenly our guide announced. 'We shall now leave the boiling sun and visit the cool tomb of Ti (pronounced 'tea').' One elderly lady who was wilting in the heat brightened up immediately. 'Oh! how nice' she cried, 'I could just do with a cup.'

Although most Chinese drink tea with their meals it is interesting to try Chinese rice wine. The best known perhaps is Shaohsing (named after a district in Chekiang province where it has been made for centuries). It is also known by other names such as Huang G'iu but most often it is known as 'Yellow Wine' because of its golden colour. Like most Chinese wines it is stored in earthenware jars and its flavour is said to be much improved after seven years and to become even better as years go by. There is a custom in the province that if a jar of the wine is buried after a baby girl is a month old, by the time of her wedding it will have aged to perfection. Most Westerners find this wine tastes like a sweet sherry. Strangely the bouquet is better when served warm. Although it is bottled it is not available abroad as it is easily spoiled.

Although rice wine is traditional, Chinese scripts relate that grape wine was introduced to China from Persia and the Mediterranean and was enjoyed so much that vines were imported from Persia about 150 BC and planted near the Emperor's Palace. Marco Polo found wine plentiful in Tai-Yuan and it is known that during the seventeenth century new vines from Turkestan were sent to the Emperor K'an-hi. A manuscript of the same century written by Chank Chao relates: 'Wine is the best dispeller of sorrows. Its name is Uncle Joy, and it has been compared to liquid jade'.

The discovery of rice wine is not so romantic. It seems that an absent-minded cook was soaking some rice in a jar and forgot about it for some time. One morning he noticed a curious smell and discovered that it came from the jar. Dipping a spoon in he found the concoction was golden in colour and he sipped a little. It was delicious and he offered it to others to taste until they were all merry and agreed more of the golden liquid must be made.

Persian poets long ago such as Firdausi, Sa'di, Hafiz and Khayyam found wine gave inspiration to their work. We get an inkling of this in Fitzgerald's translation of Omar Khayyam. Chinese poets of that era found the same thing, the only difference being that the Persian wine came from the grape, the Chinese one from rice.

Tao Ch'ien during the fourth century could not write until he had consumed a few goblets of wine and the poet Liu Lung whenever he travelled was attended by two servants, one to carry his wine and the other, obviously a strong man, to dig his grave should he die of over-indulgence. Then there was Tai Pak who one night imbibed so much he met his death by diving into a lotus pool to embrace the moon's reflection. As Confucius declares: 'There is no limit to wine drinking, but one must not get drunk'.

The strong wines, equivalent to western spirits, such as Kaoling, are distilled from grain and fruit juices such as plum and pear. One is flavoured with rose petals, again probably an innovation from Persia. Cantonese snake wine is green in colour and, as with snake soup, is held to be an excellent beverage for keeping out the cold. So is a dry wine called Great Wall.

The 'Hong Kong Cheongsam' is a cocktail consisting of gin, maraschino, white crème de menthe, fresh lemon juice, Seven-Up and egg white. A 27-year old barman won a competition with it after testing 60 alternative recipes. Leung Shiu-fai has worked at the Repulse Bay Hotel for eight years and feels he has come up with a drink worthy of representing Hong Kong abroad. It beat 120 other entries for the title in a contest organised by a local wine and spirit distributor. Of course, the real *cheongsam* is the high-necked, close fitting dress slit daringly up the sides which is sometimes worn by Chinese women. Here is the recipe for the Hong Kong Cheongsam:

1oz gin
$\frac{1}{4}$ oz maraschino
$\frac{1}{8}$ oz white crème de menthe
1 oz fresh lemon juice
$\frac{3}{4}$ oz Seven-Up
$\frac{1}{2}$ oz egg white

Shake for at least one minute and decorate with a cherry, slice of lemon, slice of cucumber and a sprig of mint.

It is firmly held in Hong Kong that, while whisky is a depressant, brandy has aphrodisiac overtones. It is not surprising, therefore, that the latter has larger sales – so large in fact that the authorities are worried. At Chinese parties wine glasses are sometimes replaced by tumblers which are half filled with the spirit. One is reminded of the debate between two inebriates, one Italian and one Chinese, about which nation produces the best lovers. The Italian said, 'You have no doubt heard of our love songs, the beauty of our women, the handsomeness of our men and our Mediterranean background.' 'Ah,' came the reply, 'but look at the size of our families'.

6 Entertainment, the Arts and Traditional Crafts

Chinese opera has a great following in Hong Kong and few visitors leave the island without attending at least one performance or part of one. It is considered quite natural to enter the auditorium at any time and leave if you have another engagement. If you get hungry while listening you can eat what you please as food is available from the attendants. You can chat with your next door neighbour if you wish or greet friends when they arrive – that is if you can be heard above the cacophony of cymbals, drums and gongs. If you shut your eyes you can imagine you are attending a noisy cocktail party. Everyone has an enjoyable time and even children attend. The commotion may seem somewhat confusing but there are many fascinating things about Chinese opera to enjoy.

The operatic costumes are elaborate, colourful and exquisitely made. The headdresses are even more ornate and gleaming with artificial jewels of fantastic size. Cloaks and royal robes are made of silk and satin, richly embroidered with threads of gold, artificial gemstones and sequins. Various colours indicate the status of the different roles in the opera. For instance, yellow is the colour of emperors, green represents a person of high rank, and purple is the mark of the general.

There are two styles of opera, Cantonese and Pekingese. The latter is in Mandarin dialect in high-pitched falsetto using very heavy make-up, a derivation from the time when all the players used masks. The stage is almost bare. Sometimes a chair and a table might serve as a hill, a lookout post or perhaps a tower and the brandishing of a tasseled switch indicates horse riding. Only in very recent years have women played the female roles in Pekingese opera. Formerly it was felt that the stage was an entirely unsuitable place for women, so all female roles were portrayed by men.

Many years of intensive study go into the making of an opera star.

In Hong Kong, training is carried out privately and includes a strenuous daily schedule of singing practice and a run-through of the all-important eye and hand movements. There is a good deal of personal dedication and self-sacrifice involved: one famous singer is said to have soaked her hands in water for hours each day for many years to make them pliable and give them the desired translucent effect. Plots come from history or legend; goodness always triumphs over evil, and it is easy to know who is the villain or wicked ogre by their costumes and make-up.

Today, Hong Kong's Chinese opera enthusiasts can enjoy free performances in the parks and playgrounds, where the Urban Council runs a year-round series of open-air Cantonese and Peking-ese performances. For instance, there are nightly operas at Lai Chi Koh amusement park. Take a 6A bus from the Kowloon Star Ferry terminal. Whether you enjoy it or not, it is as real or unreal as Disneyland and an experience not met with elsewhere except in Taiwan or mainland China.

Should you happen to be on a shopping spree late on a Wednesday in the Ocean Centre/Ocean Terminal complex in Kowloon there is a treat in store for you. Between 6 and 7 p.m. the Hong Kong Tourist Association and the Hong Kong and Kowloon Wharf and Godown Co. Ltd present an entertainment which offers the visitor some insight into China's cultural heritage. There are nine separate programmes which are performed in rotation: Chinese instrumental music; Fukienese glove puppet show; Chinese folk songs and dances; Chinese acrobatic and magic shows; martial arts demonstration; Fukienese folk dances; Cantonese rod puppet show; Cantonese opera and demonstration; Chinese folk choral singing

Should the idea of a miniature Chinese opera group sound appealing, the puppet theatre is for you. Hong Kong has three types of puppets, those held by hands, sticks or rods. The latter are the most unusual and there is one troupe in Hong Kong, run by Mak Shiu-Tong, affectionately referred to as 'the grand old man of puppetry', for he has been in the business for over 50 years. The rod puppet's neck is fitted on an oval piece of wood, forming the shoulders which holds the costume. Under this a tiny shirt is also held by the shoulders affixed to a pair of puppet hands by long sticks. The right hand of the puppeteer grasps the neck stick under the costume and the left manipulates the arm sticks. The puppets are clad in magnificent silken and embroidered robes patterned like those of the Cantonese opera down to the last sequin. Also their headdresses and heavy make-up is exactly like the characters they imitate.

5 Ceiling of Miu Fat Temple in the New Territories.

6 Miu Fat Temple.

7 Lok Ma Chau look-out over China from the New Territories.

8 LEFT Taiwanese celebration of the anniversary of Confucius' birth in the year 552 B.C. It is a national holiday.

9 BELOW LEFT Formal Taiwanese costume, called *chi pao*.
10 BELOW RIGHT The marble gorge of Taroko.

17 Chinese opera performer.

18 This traditionally attired group of Hong Kong musicians, Jing Ying, has toured several countries, bringing Chinese music to Western audiences.

Mak Shiu-Tong and his troupe are frequently invited to give outdoor presentations and they are always delighted to explain the history of their craft to anyone who is interested. Chinese puppets are said to have originated during the Han dynasty (207 BC) when their principal role was not played on the stage but in tombs! Made in the life-size image of a human, with head, body and the basic mechanics of movement, the puppet was an important part of funeral services, symbolising the protector of the dead person's soul against the entry of evil spirits. Superstition still exists about puppets to this day. They are individually wrapped and stored in big red boxes for it is believed that open-eyed puppets could be possessed by evil spirits if they are not hidden away during their idle moments.

For visitors who may wish to buy them, the China Products company sell glove and string versions. They are sold at the Yee Tung crafts village in the Excelsior Hotel shopping arcade and at the Mountain Folkcraft shop in Kowloon's Ocean Terminal shopping complex.

Hong Kong has a professional symphony orchestra with some 70 players and a Chinese one with traditional Chinese instruments including the lute-like pi-pa with a resonant, delicate timbre, two-string violins, bamboo pipe mouth organs and double reed instruments. Modern Chinese music, based on elementary western techniques, is apt to sound superficial to western ears. Some compositions however such as the Yellow River and Butterfly Lover's concertos (the latter a score for violin and orchestra based on well-known operatic themes), do enjoy considerable popularity. The Jing Ting orchestra which appears in traditional costume has toured a number of western countries.

On most days of the week it is possible to find live jazz at some of Hong Kong's bars and restaurants. Many record shops offer a wide range of imported jazz records at attractive prices and jazz is a regular feature of Hong Kong's major annual cultural event, the Hong Kong Arts Festival. The centre of jazz activity is to be found on Sunday afternoons in Causeway Bay in, of all unlikely places the Excelsior Hotel's Dickens Bar. Here, within the wood pannelled-walls lined with cartoons of Dickens's characters, a seven-piece combo, Tony Carpio and his Friends, entertain. Guitarist Carpio is one of Hong Kong's most experienced musicians. He has played in the United States where he developed a swinging and articulate jazz solo style, and in Hong Kong is in constant demand as an orchestra leader and musical director. Another star in the group is trombonist Omeng Alarcon, a cheery personality whose enthusiasm for his music is

19 A Hong Kong musician with a pi-pa. This lute-like instrument has a resonant delicate timbre.

always evident. Omeng spends his days working in television studios and his spare time blowing some of the finest jazz to be heard in Hong Kong.

In contrast to the plush comfort of the Dickens Bar are the more spartan surroundings of Ned Kelly's Last Stand, an Australian-owned pub on the Kowloon side of Hong Kong harbour. Once through the batwing doors the visitor exchanges the oriental scene outside for the dimly lit austerity of a popular jazz haunt that is as near to home for visitors as anywhere in the East. The walls are decorated with faded 'wanted' notices for the notorious Ned and photographs of famous Australian cricket players.

Many of the entertainments which we enjoy and take for granted today have their origin in the old Imperial court in Peking. In addition to their love of music and a fascination with puppetry, the Emperors delighted in acrobats with their antics on the top of poles and their tight rope walking. Magicians who had hitherto confined their skills to foretelling the future, developed their conjuring art. Actors and actresses were known as 'The children of the Pear Garden' because it was the site of the Imperial drama school, founded by Emperor Ming-Huang during the colourful Tang Dynasty. Unbelievably, there were chess playing crows, trained butterflies, bees and crickets. Small wonder that little finches can tell fortunes today.

As has been said, magicians had existed for many hundreds of years before that dynasty, shrouded in a cloak of mystery and regarded by most people as sorcerers. Although references are elusive, one document tells of a magician who claimed to have discovered the secret of immortality which he sold in the form of a pill. It would be interesting to know the ingredients. Yet other accounts mention fortunes being made in temples where worshippers were deceived by means of skilful illusion.

Chu's Magic Studio at 401 Chatham Road in Kowloon has clients all over the world. Among the magic items for sale are a deluxe dagger chest, an oriental inexhaustible chest, multiplying candles, and a portable head chopper! These and many other tricks are also available at two 'magic effects' counters at the Matsuzakaya Department Store and at the Yee Tung Village, both in Causeway Bay.

Among the most talented dancers in Hong Kong are the Miramar Classical Dance Troupe. Formed in 1958 they have 30 members and appear twice nightly at the Miramar Theatre restaurant where diners are entertained by Chinese floor shows. Among the dances performed is the 'Fairy Dance' where one artiste dances as a fairy in a sea palace.

Waves are represented by the ballerina with ribbons. Another ribbon dance is performed by several members of the troupe twirling long coloured ribbons into constantly changing shapes. The dance with two swords is, as the name suggests, a most dramatic and dangerous spectacle. The story tells of the final moments of Yue Kay, lover of the Warlord of Chu who fought against the founder of the Han Dynasty for control of the Empire. The Warlord, one of the most colourful characters in Chinese history, lost the struggle and took his own life. Yue Kay followed him to death and performed this final dance before killing herself with a sword. The 'Victor's Return' depicts a duel between two generals, a display of martial arts performed before the Emperor by two generals just returned from a victorious war. The costumes are spectacular and the weapons impressive.

A visit to Hong Kong is not complete without seeing a Dragon or a Lion dance – preferably both. A Dragon dance is always performed during festivals or on special occasions. A dignitary is invited to 'dot' the eye, a great honour, which brings the dragon to life and is done with a black paint brush. Once this ceremony is over the dragon starts to move sinuously along the streets between admiring crowds to the sound of clashing cymbals, the beating of drums and gongs and the explosions of firecrackers. Dragons vary in length some being as much as 140 feet (43 metres) long. Their reptilian skins made of cloth are held overhead by young men on a skeleton of bamboo sticks and poles. The number of people that make up a dragon depends on its length and he assumes a very fierce demeanour as his body goes up and down, twists and turns while the men run and keep raising and lowering their arms. The dragon may look ferocious but at least he does not breathe flames, and his progress is cheered by young and old.

The Lion Dance is also performed on special occasions and he is a better dancer than a dragon because he is not as long and is controlled by only two men. One holds up the head and the other man grasps him beneath the fabric skin, around the waist.

Usually the two men are dancers or acrobats and, with perfect co-ordination can simulate many changes of mood. He can be playful, prance, gambol, jump, play with a ball and even dance. He can appear contented or very fierce, depending on his mood. Again the dance is accompanied by music and firecrackers which sometimes frighten him. Some lion heads are beautiful with long tawny manes, large docile eyes and drooping mouths while others show their teeth in anger and growl. Whatever the lion's mood people do not crowd too closely to him!

In the past, the film industry in Hong Kong was overshadowed by those of its neighbours in Japan and India. Most of the pictures in those early days were in the Cantonese dialect and focused on themes directly related to local life. They were churned out in great numbers (film schedules of a fortnight were not uncommon) and what they lacked in quality they made up for in zest. In fact, it was the same story as occurred in early Hollywood days.

The Hong Kong film industry began making its first real impact in the post-war period when companies started catering for a rapidly increasing population. This enabled them to have bigger budgets and produce movies which sold throughout south-east Asia. The emphasis switched to Mandarin pictures with broader appeal – romances, comedies, costume dramas and sword-play epics. They showed more care in their preparation and, although they still exhibited little in the way of innovation, they helped launch several of the studios. The troubles that afflicted the large studios in Hollywood and Britain during the 'sixties did not occur to any great extent in Hong Kong where the emphasis remained on simplicity and consolidation.

As the industry moved into the 'seventies, however, several events occurred to turn the spotlight on the Hong Kong movie industry and pave the way for future advances and its current competitiveness. The first and probably best known, was the rise of a local actor to the ranks of superstardom throughout the world. His name: Bruce Lee. Kung Fu, a Chinese martial arts technique, had been a popular subject for motion pictures in Hong Kong for many years and hardly a week would pass without two or three such shows being screened to large, approving audiences. Bruce Lee, aided by a canny producer/partner, transformed it into a world-wide fad. Before his untimely death in 1973, his popularity had spawned a dozen imitators, stimulated other movie-makers to cash in on the craze with efforts of their own and, most significantly, brought recognition to the Hong Kong movie industry.

Another step toward the industry's increasing maturity came with the first attempts at making shows in collaboration with well-established studios from the United States and Britain. The success of this cooperation prompted even larger budget epics. The improved standard of living in Hong Kong enabled these to be paid for and they were successfully exported. By 1980 the movie industry was flushed with success and business had never been better. *Enter the Dragon* with Bruce Lee was listed by *Variety*, the trade magazine, as one of the 50 top-grossing films of all time. Of the smaller studios and producers King Hu won a prize at the 1975 Cannes Film Festival with

A Touch of Zen. The number of cinemas in Hong Kong increased to 80 and in spite of rises in admission charges to a top price of about US$2.00 per ticket, attendance figures also rose to 65 million. Golden Harvest, the company which backed Bruce Lee, has undertaken perhaps the most ambitious programme. It proposes to supplement its local output by producing some major films involving big box office stars and crews for overseas release. The scene is dominated by Golden Harvest and Shaw Brothers but they do not have the field to themselves. A dozen or so other smaller studios are also taking steps to branch out internationally, either with joint efforts or full production in other countries, from Morocco to Alaska. Some of the work will be done at home. As one mogul explained: 'Hong Kong now has everything needed to put a production company together, just as is done in Hollywood. We can do it ourselves with our own capital and we can even do it for others. All they have to do is bring the production nucleus and we can supply the rest.'

One sideline of the film industry proving extremely profitable is the production of television commercials for use in many countries. Some 90 per cent of households own at least one television set and watching it has become, as in other countries, one of the island's principal leisure pastimes. There are three stations, two being commercial, while the third, Radio-Television Hong Kong, is government owned. This last ranks drama and documentaries among their top viewing time. Of the two radio stations, the government one broadcasts in English, the commercial one in both English and Chinese. If your time is short in Hong Kong you can get a very good idea of what you can purchase and where from commercials on the television set in your bedroom.

China has a long tradition in the field of fine arts and has always been associated with objets d'art of great beauty and craftsmen of infinite skill and patience. Of the many products to come out of China, those that are the most famous must surely be jade, ivory, lacquer ware and porcelain.

The Chinese have valued jade above all other semi-precious stones for thousands of years, referring to it as 'quintessence of heaven and earth'. It is believed that its lovely colour, silky feel and beauty confer on it the power to ward off danger and disease. In the Imperial Court of China it was obligatory for a nobleman to have a jade insignia, and his rank was judged by his amulets and charms of jade. The Emperor had an exquisite imperial jade seal, baton and sceptre blade. The altar at which he worshipped, and even the sandals he wore, were all of jade. Royal records were inscribed on jade and stored in

20 A well-known director of Shaw Brothers directing a Ching Dynasty period film at the famous 'movie city' in Clear Water Bay.

sandalwood boxes tied with slender cords of gold. An Emperor of the T'ang Dynasty (AD 618–906), Huan-Tsung, is said to have presented a magnificent jade bed to his favourite concubine. The third-century classical scholar, Wang Su, recorded that Confucius spoke of jade in terms of virtues – the smooth surface suggesting gentleness of character, its fine texture, wisdom, and its solidity, duty to one's neighbour. During China's Ming Dynasty it was believed that a drink composed of finely ground, fresh jade relieved asthma and kept one's hair glossy – when taken in the correct doses.

Jade consists of two different minerals, jadeite and nephrite, and though green is the colour identified with it, it also comes in lovely shades of pink, red, yellow, brown, mauve, turquoise and milk-white, which is the rarest. The true test of an authentic piece of jade, say the experts, is its hardness. For where the tip of a penknife will leave a scratch mark on imitation jade, the genuine remains unharmed.

The Chinese have been carving ivory for centuries and lovely old pieces can still be bought, but it is difficult for the ordinary person to tell exactly how old a beautiful object is because it is so easy to age the material and, indeed, imitate it in plastic. This does at least satisfy those people who are worried about the decimation of elephant herds. Increasingly strict conservation laws are reducing the stocks of ivory, so the law of supply and demand is pushing up the cost. However, it has been known for hundreds of years that the tusks from a North African male elephant yield the finest ivory while the North African female comes a close second. The Indian elephant does not have such magnificent tusks and the female none at all. Genuine ivory has concentric veins like a tree trunk and although these should distinguish it from plastic, even they can be cleverly counterfeited. However, it is still possible to pick up authentic ivory pieces at the market stalls, such as beautifully carved fans, combs, figures, ornaments and those fascinating carved concentric balls each detached from the other yet one inside each other. A dedicated gourmet will tell you that food never tastes so delicious as when eaten with real ivory chopsticks. Most antique dealers have lovely old ivory carvings and sometimes exquisite fans cut and pierced whose blades slide together like silk – but all will be expensive if genuine. Lacquer work has undergone constant development and is one of China's best-known crafts, its origin going back far into antiquity. Articles are covered with the sap of the lacquer tree which is applied as a protective coating. It dries as a hard varnish and further layers are then applied in various colours.

The Chou dynasty became so famous in the craft that lacquer trees were formally cultivated, and their caretakers even had a place in the bureaucracy. Lacquer was used in ever-wider applications – from dishes to boats, chariots and weapons of various kinds – making them not only more beautiful but also more durable. The art advanced significantly during the T'ang dynasty (AD 618–907), and several new techniques were invented during this period. One was the appliqúing of gold and silver, designs which were cut out of thin sheets of these metals and embedded in the lacquer surface, which was then polished. Another T'ang technique was lacquer carving, in which a thick coating of numerous layers of lacquer was built up on the surface of the piece, and designs were then carved into this coating. Red lacquer was most often used for this process, but there are also examples in black and yellow. This technique was also successfully used with layers of different coloured lacquers, in which various parts of the design were cut to the depth of the desired colour layer. This polychrome carving technique produced beautiful motifs of flowers, vegetation, clouds and mountains. There is a superb collection of lacquer work in the National Palace Museum in Taiwan.

The Chinese have been making porcelain for many centuries and we acknowledge the association between the craft and China by naming our tableware after that country.

Jingdezhen was well known for its porcelain at the beginning of the eleventh century, but it was the Ming dynasty of the fifteenth century which saw the first production of the exquisite blue and white wares. More potteries were set up and, eventually, it found its way to Europe via Persia, where I saw superb examples a few years ago. So the Chinese – perhaps the greatest potters ever known – inspired faience artists in Europe. At Delft, by the seventeenth century, Dutch potters had managed to reproduce the two colours, if not the translucent porcelain itself. The latter was possible in Jingdezhen because of the exceptional kaolin clay found in the district. I did not see any blue and white pottery being made in Hong Kong but did so in Holland, and it is interesting that before the glazing and firing, the famous Delft Blue is a dull green but turns blue during the process. Porcelain ginger jars and tea caddies have long been associated with China and, another collectors' piece are the beautiful and traditional porcelain pillows. These come in different shapes and sizes since they were used by all age groups, from quite young children to elderly people. They are smaller than ordinary pillows, rectangular in shape with a concave side for the neck. At one time these were obligatory and aristocratic families always slept on their backs. Posture was all important as it still is and the right size pillow ensured that it was maintained even while asleep. The pillows also helped to preserve the elaborate hairstyles as they were not disturbed in this sleeping position. Another present-day collectors' piece came about because, in no circumstances would ladies in high-born families undress for a doctor. Instead they had beautiful naked china dolls on which they could indicate the position of their malady. The necessary prescription was then made out. It is possible that this reticence may have been the cause of acupuncture. It was discovered that insertions into specific parts of the body could cure or relieve pains in another area. Over the centuries it has become a very sophisticated art and is now accepted by the medical profession in many countries. It was originally practised with bamboo splinters but today fine pointed needles, preferably of silver and of varying lengths and thicknesses, are used. The insertion of the needles must be absolutely precise, sometimes said to be exactly between nerve endings. Whatever the acupuncturist's skill, it is extremely complicated to learn and first of all involves usual precedures such as pulse-taking. The needles are often vibrated or rotated and sometimes dipped in herbs before use. It is difficult to assess if there is an element of faith healing or perhaps whether it is something to do with the body's basic forces of energy. Certainly it does produce some amazing cures and can even replace an anaesthetic.

As chemist shops flourish in the West so do those of the herbalists in any shopping district in Hong Kong. Some of the mixtures are very complicated and expensive, others simple and very reasonable in price, such as buying a little ginger to use as a disinfectant to rub into freshly pierced ear lobes. People's opinions differ as to which cures are really effective, but many have their favourites and perhaps there is an element of faith healing here too. A popular belief is that an extract from tiger bones is considered good for treating rheumatism. The bones are reduced to a form of pure carbon by heating them gently over a period of time, but the process and labour involved is intensive, therefore expensive in affluent Hong Kong, and is tending to price itself out of existence.

Deer's horn, some of it from as far a field as New Zealand, West Germany and Britain, is ground up and mixed with honey as a cure for fever. The tail and sex organs are believed to act as an aphrodisiac, as indeed is the lengendary horn of the rhinoceros. Fossilised bones and animal teeth are ground up for inclusion in many prescriptions. Mixed with date kernels they are used as a tranquilliser or a cure for insomnia. The treatment is claimed to have no side effects.

Western researchers, knowing how complicated mixtures can be, have been surprised to find that quantities of quite ordinary health-giving plants are also used by Chinese herbalists. These include wild mint, liquorice root, chrysanthemum flowers, cloves and the leaves of the gingko tree. The latter have proved surprisingly effective in fighting colds.

There are many other ingredients strongly recommended by the herbalists which Westerners find hard to accept – or swallow. The most controversial is ginseng. Shops stock some 30 varieties of this expensive root from the much-prized 'red' ginseng exported in airtight cans from North Korea, to the cheaper 'white' ginseng harvested in the north-western United States. There is also an extremely rare wild ginseng grown on a high mountain in north-east China. The area is perpetually covered with snow, and the root must be dug from the frozen ground with wooden tools as if metal might somehow detract from its life-giving properties. One piece as big as your little finger can cost thousands of dollars. It is carefully stored in cellars between layers of fried rice which are changed every two months to avoid decay. This particular ginseng is too expensive for anything but emergency use. A dying man may want all his children around his death bed. Some might be a few days' travelling away. The wild root is boiled in chicken broth and given to the patient to keep him alive long enough to assemble the entire family. Many Western authorities dismiss such claims and declare ginseng has no more stimulant value than raw carrot, but millions of Chinese think otherwise.

An alternative compound made of ground fossils, is said to stop excessive sweating. The fossils come from China where the authorities are alarmed at the possible destruction of valuable scientific evidence of the distant past. Further exports are now forbidden. The bones of Peking man, a forerunner of *homo sapiens* discovered in 1927 in a cave near the capital, vanished a few days after Pearl Harbour. It is feared these priceless relics may have been turned into medicine.

Seashells, even pearls, are used to a certain extent. Carefully ground, they are used in tranquilliser compounds. Minerals, like mercury, are also prescribed, though generally for external application.

A species of hornet, known in Cantonese as *Sim Toi*, swarms across south China during the lychee harvest. Thousands are attracted to their death in vats of sugered water. The bugs are then sun-dried and stored. With head, sting, claws and legs removed, their dried bodies are mixed with herbs to cure children of influenza or even, in some cases, of fear of the dark.

A herbal dealer's skills go beyond the preparation of prescriptions. Inferior substitutes are always appearing on the market. This is especially true of ginseng. Unscrupulous producers have been known to dye the root and pass it off as the highest priced variety. Equipment is more modern in herbalists shops today. Stone mortars are still used, but sadly plastic containers have replaced the wooden boxes and glass bottles.

Fortune-telling holds great sway in Hong Kong. It includes face and palm reading, fortune sticks and tiny birds. Small fragile sticks like tapers are shaken inside a cylindrical container until one pops out. From a number on this the future can be told. Palm reading is universally known but face reading is not. The expert in this by studying from forehead to eyebrow can read the past, from eyebrow to the tip of the nose what happens in middle life and from nose to chin what is about to happen. Visitors may be a bit apprehensive about this, but nearly everyone is fascinated by the small bird method of fortune-telling. A pack of cards is spread on a table and the door of a cage is opened to allow a small bird to hop over the pack and select a card in its beak. From this card the client's future can be foretold!

Another art for which the Chinese are famous is calligraphy, and the drawing of these pictorial characters is a highly skilful and relaxing pastime. You will find plenty of opportunities to watch it being done and derive pleasure from it even though you do not understand it. Artists have different ways of forming the characters but always seem to hold the brush in the same stereotyped manner with the thumb and four fingers, never touching the paper with the hand. It dates back more than 5000 years. The characters are formed from left to right in rows or vertically, and great originality and personality are displayed, although it always retains its traditional style. In ancient times scrolls were used, but today you can buy calligraphy in rectangular, square or narrow formats and it is used to decorate ribbons and other materials. Each time a new shop opens the entrance is hung with paper flowers intertwined with silken ribbons covered with characters. Different brushes are used to give various effects: wide characters are achieved most easily with a brush of wolf fur, while a thinner line needs a more delicate brush of goat's wool with a centre of wolf fur. A calligrapher will paint your name or anything you like and he can be found in shopping centres, on sightseeing boats and sometimes on the pavement before a tiny square table waiting patiently, like a letter writer. There are still a few of these about, even today, waiting to help the less literate send greetings or tell the news to a relative on the mainland.

Quite a different kind of script is used by those who are gifted mediums and can do automatic writing. Unlike the West, ordinary pens and paper are not used. Instead, an instrument, held by the medium, is almost like a small water diviner's stick cut from a willow or peach tree. The base of the Y is carved to resemble a dragon's head and then gilded. This is held above what looks like a small card table whose top is a shallow tray covered with rice, sand or the ashes of incense. Mediums can often be found in temples who will obtain messages from a special god on behalf of the consultant. Sometimes the answer comes in poetic form or sometimes the god will not reply at all. Golden paper money can be burned to appease a god who remains silent.

Nothing can be quite as fascinating for someone who loves paintings as slowly unrolling a Chinese handpainted scroll. Perhaps it begins at the source of a river and, as it is unfolded, more of the river becomes visible, it broadens through plains, narrows and deepens through gorges and either empties into the sea, or vanishes into the distance. Each time you unfurl it you imagine you might and perhaps do, see something you have not noticed before. In landscape scenes the clouds half hiding the mountains are merely suggested, not painted, but the sky behind them gives an illusion of endless space. Movement is suggested by birds, animals and flowers and occasionally you may find a figure of a shepherd or someone in the distance coming towards the front of the painting. Each view has a story which the artist has seen and you can see and enjoy differently.

Before the invention of paper the Chinese artist painted on silk but once paper had been invented, during the T'ang dynasty, it was commonly used, although it never had the artistic value of silk. China still produces handmade paper which is second to none. Excellent paper which was reasonably durable was made from the pith of a special plant but it had to be treated with care. For some reason it has always been known in the West as 'rice' paper, although that is not its source. The method of production is similar to that used in the manufacture of plywood. The stems of the plant are first soaked in water and then rotated against a broad sharp blade so that the cylinder is unrolled into a continuous sheet of constant thickness which is then dried. Its chief advantage is its intense whiteness but it is fragile and must either be pasted onto a backing, sometimes of silk, or at least have the edges reinforced with ribbon. Sets of a few paintings could be bound together in a fabric album, smaller ones being stored in ornate boxes. Some were almost miniatures, the size of playing cards and came in even smaller boxes as a gift. An artist painting on such a small surface with tiny brushes would use the cushion of the thumb as a palette. Nowadays they are collectors' items but many were made because they could be copied. The 'rice' paper was so thin that a light behind it allowed an artist to trace the picture through and the new outline could be coloured by other artists who were specialists in certain types of flora and fauna.

The Chinese have always loved fans and until a few years ago men enjoyed using them as much as women. They were not only fashionable but could conceal a stilleto in their folds or tiny mirrors in which people could be observed without realising it. Their shape is attractive whether it be but a palm leaf on a bamboo stick or made of ivory delicately pierced or fretted. Another variant is made of sandalwood. The framework is usually scored with designs in relief using red hot points or painted with figures or landscapes. Some have a narrow strip of silk on which there will be painted birds, flowers or fish. Whatever the design, when you unfurl it you will be rewarded with the refreshing scent of sandalwood.

Copies of engravings can often be bought which date back to the turn of the century and are not only delightful to own but easy to carry in your aircraft luggage. They are sold in sets of four or six and show what Hong Kong looked like in the early days. There are equally beautiful ones of Macau from original engravings published in the early 1800s. They show some of the architectural features and life style of that period. Six prints are packed in a specially designed gift box with a brief history of the scenes.

Not many people stationed in Hong Kong return home without bringing some Chinese furniture amongst their belongings. Scrolled and round legged cocktail tables can be found in many English houses and collectors' pieces add to the beauty of drawing rooms and halls. Antique furniture shops are crowded with visitors or expatriots seeking treasures, perhaps in 'Canton Provincial Style'.

'Blackwood' chairs, tables and chests are usually made in fact of lacquered and varnished redwoods, stained black. This colour is not only considered stately but the finish protects against humidity. Redwood chairs with marble seats and backs, known as *Da Li*, not only look attractive but were also made with weather in mind because they are cool to sit on. The marble has an ascetic appeal with its varied colour and veining which, when polished, sometimes suggests landscapes. 'Altar' tables, placed at one time beneath ancestral family portraits, are sought by many. These often have ornately carved legs and turned up edges. There are folding tables, small platform couches and all kinds of chairs, most of the antique ones with a rail between the front legs near the floor so that high-born ladies could rest their tiny bound feet and keep them off cold floors.

Should you be fortunate to fall in love with one of the massive 'opium bed' couches, they were made so that they could be dismantled, because of their size. The first time I ever saw one of these was in a Taiwan museum and I was impressed by the number of people it could accommodate. Not only are these couches very long but they are also deep from back to front and were made so that many people could sit together with their legs tucked up.

Ming chairs can cost a fortune and if you do not see one in the shops you can at least admire them in museums. The backs, legs and arms are delicately carved and joined together with wooden pegs to allow for expansion and contraction in changing temperatures. Made of dark brown sandalwood the finished chair becomes an exotic deep purple. This is achieved by soaking the wood beforehand in oil and, when this is absorbed and polished, the finished article is as smooth as silk to the touch.

Camphor trees are abundant in the New Territories and one of the best selling pieces of furniture for many years has been chests made of the wood. They are delicately carved perhaps with landscapes, or less ornate ones with flowers. Camphor wood has a distinctive smell and repels moths and woodworm more efficiently than chemicals, so when you wish to pack your winter clothes away for the summer a camphor wood chest is the answer and it can easily be shipped home.

For devotees of antique joinery some good has come out of the endemic Hong Kong destruction and reconstruction. Recently a 95-year-old building came under the axe. It contained an old-style apothecary's shop lined with drawers, shelves laden with jars and bottles and the usual locked cupboard for poisons. This has been dismantled and reassembled in a new museum. It is reminiscent of the medieval pharmacy in Bruges (Belgium), since the Middle Ages part of St John's Hospital, and now also turned into a museum. There you can see the tools of the apothecary's trade long ago: the lovely old porcelain jars which used to contain herbs and mixtures, silver pestles and mortars; also a great, elbow-high, wooden counter beneath which drawers with labels in latin slide in and out as smoothly as the day they were finished.

7 Sports and Pastimes

The most popular form of recreation in Hong Kong is race-going. The Chinese love of horses is well known and dates back to the time when the Mongols formed their first cavalry divisions. Statues of these early horses are still greatly admired in museums for their robust, sturdy appearance. The Happy Valley Race Course was formed in the 1840s and in 1884, with a view to better racing, the Hong Kong Jockey Club was formed and took over control. Things did not go easily; heavy rains flooded the race course and damaged the original bamboo stand. It was replaced by a solid wooden structure. All went well for several years until 1918 when tragedy struck. Perhaps there was too great a crowd for the stand, the exact cause is not known, but it collapsed and even that was not the end of the disaster. The stoves in the kitchens beneath were crushed, set light to the woodwork and the flames spread so quickly that in the holocaust 600 lives were lost. New stands were not completed for over a decade but, by 1937, there were two seven-storey buildings and these were eventually expanded to the viewing stands of today.

The Chinese are great race-goers and many of the meetings take place in the evenings under powerful flood lighting. Attendance at one of these occasions seems slightly unreal to the Westerner with the high-rise residential blocks round the course providing additional viewing space to the vast stand.

From the beginning the Jockey Club has been a strictly non profit-making organisation that benefits charity and, in 1960, in recognition of this generosity, Queen Elizabeth II granted the 'Royal' prefix. The money bet on horses enables the club to help 180 organisations; indeed 75 per cent of totalisator takings go to charity. The racing season is from September to May. Visitors may obtain admission badges for the Members' Enclosure on a first come, first served basis, up to 10 a.m. on the day of the meeting, from the Hong Kong Tourist Office.

Now there is a second racecourse in the New Territories at Shatin. It has been built on 243 acres (97 hectares) reclaimed from the sea and was opened in 1978 – the Chinese year of the Horse. The stables are air-conditioned and there is even a nine-foot deep swimming pool for the horses. At both courses enormous matrix television screens in front of the stands enable race-goers to see the exact position of the horse at any point in the circuit.

Besides loving horses, the Chinese are great gamblers and betting at the race track and the sale of lottery tickets are big business. Casinos are not allowed in Hong Kong, but the Chinese more than make up for it when they go to Macau. There are several golden rules to learn when in the casinos: do not stand behind a loser as he may think you are the cause of his bad luck; never tap a gambler on his shoulder while he is playing as that is sure to bring him bad luck; if you yourself wish to be a winner do not have your hair cut before you enter a casino.

Other outlets for the Chinese love of gambling are card games such as Fan Tan, Chinese chess and mah-jong. It is said the Chinese will even bet on flies walking up a window pane. I am not an addict to these types of games and it has always struck me as odd that people can be out of doors with all kinds of interesting things round them yet while away their time playing such games. On a recent visit to the tombs of Sakkara in Egypt our guide became quite worried when he lost three of his clients. He found them sitting by some ruins and they looked up with welcoming smiles as he approached them. One Englishman was dealing out cards on a flat stone slab to the other two people and said cheerily 'We don't think we'll see the other tombs now. Would you like to join us for a game of bridge?'

Some days later during a Nile cruise we were watching feluccas sailing into the sunset when a American lady said how much she had enjoyed sight seeing in the warm weather ashore that day but would I now join a bridge table below deck. I was able to reply truthfully that I did not know how to play bridge but, next evening, after she and several others had remained on board while the rest of us had visited Abu Simbel, it dawned on me how fanatical about games some people can become. The more so the next morning when I heard her say as she gazed at the great temple ashore, 'I can now put in my diary that I have visited Abu Simbel!'

Chinese chess or *Hsieng C'hi*, has a big following in Hong Kong and

21 Chinese chess playing is a common scene in most public parks and gardens on any fine day in Hong Kong.

22 A Chinese chess board with all the 32 chess pieces in position.

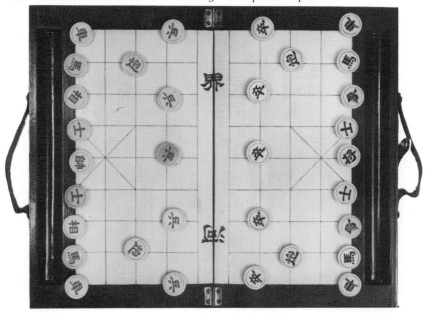

you can watch it, as I have said before, in the public parks and gardens. It is a cheap game now but used to be the preserve of the Emperor and his ministers as a means of fortune telling. Later, scholars and those with political ambitions, realised it could further their careers.

A simple set with a folded paper board and pieces made of the cheapest wood sells for as little as HK$2 while one with its own wooden board and matching pieces can cost about HK$15. Also available are elaborate chess sets carved of ivory or jade which could fetch a fortune. The board has 64 squares, divided by a blank space – the river. There are 16 pieces in each camp, comprising a general, two ministers, two elephants, two horses, two chariots, two cannon and five soldiers.

Who can tell which is the most popular in Hong Kong, chess or mah-jong? It seems you see more people playing the latter in Hong Kong but the former is preferred in Macau. Certainly mah-jong makes a noise and people seem to be philosophical when playing it and what an attractive game it is to watch. Each of the four players has a wall of tiles concealed from the others and they make attractive patterns as they play. Shades of the Great Wall! Most of the tiles these days are made of plastic but the connoisseur enjoys the feel of real ivory and sandalwood. It is claimed that mah-jong is not a game to the Chinese but a social attribute, despite the clacking of the tiles – indeed to many the sound is musical.

Bird fancying is another popular pastime in Hong Kong. The Chinese have a special reverence for birds, because it is thought that they suggest free souls, and you will often see bird cages being carried about. If you watch closely you will notice that the cage is gently swung so that the bird has to fluff its feathers and spread its wings to keep its balance on the perch. This gives it exercise and the bird enjoys the fresh air. One bird fancier has six birds in separate cages and gives over a room in his tiny flat to them. Early each morning he takes one cage out for a walk before his breakfast. The following morning another one, and so on through the week. On Sundays he takes them all out, two at a time, one in each hand. Bird fanciers extol the virtues of their pets to other bird fanciers and there are even restaurants where you can take your bird cage along when you eat.

Mention in this book has been made several times of shadow boxing or *Tai Chi Chuan* the Chinese art of calisthenics – literal English translation, 'the Great Ultimate Fist'. You will see people outdoors and even on roof tops going through the slow-motion, ritual movements with total concentration, quite unaware of any audience.

Its origin dates back more than 1000 years and is said to have been started by a Taoist priest named Cheung Sam-Fung after watching a fight to the death between a snake and a bird.

The bird started a vigorous onslaught on the snake by swooping down from a tree but the serpent evaded the attacks time and again by coiling itself so as to present no vulnerable target. Finally the bird tired and relaxed and the snake struck back. So accurate was its venomous aim that the bird was killed instantly. Religion barred the priests from carrying weapons so Sam-Fung evolved the method he had seen for self-defence, as priests in those turbulent days were often the targets of robbers. There are movements with such names as 'catching the peacock's tail', 'playing the guitar', and even 'finding a needle at the bottom of the sea'. Apart from being a method of self defence, the slow rhythmical and controlled breathing involved is said to relax taut nerves, improve the functioning of the internal organs and stimulate the blood circulation.

If you are a bird watcher, then the New Territories offer ample opportunity to indulge your hobby. Perhaps the egret is the easiest to spot as he is seen constantly following the plough to catch the worms that are thrown up and his pure white feathers can be seen from a distance against the green grass or dark earth. Ospreys dive for fish, pelicans are numerous as are spoonbills. Hong Kong lies on the migration route across the China coast as the birds fly south. The Hong Kong Bird Watching Society which conducts full and half day expeditions and the Hong Kong Tourist Association can give you details.

Should you be interested in shell collecting, Mirs Bay in the New Territories, has good sandy beaches with patches of coral. There is a Hong Kong Shell Society which, on the last Sunday in each month, organises trips, and indoor meetings are held on the last Monday of every month at 6.30 p.m.

For golf enthusiasts, there are several courses to choose from. There is one at Shek O on Hong Kong Island, and in the New Territories three 18-hole courses at Fanling, a 9-hole course at Deepwater Bay, and a new one is being built at Clearwater Bay in the eastern New Territories together with a country club. It should be a going concern by the time you read this, and among the more unusual champion-ships courses. Set on a rocky peninsula several hundred feet above sea level, each hole will have a view of the sea and outlying islands. It is arranged on two levels with the first nine holes – the 'Mountain Course' – accessible by escalator and rising to a height of 470 feet. The back nine – the 'Ocean Course' – ranges in altitude from 75 to 243 feet

23 A familiar early morning sight in one of Hong Kong's many public areas where *Tai Chi Chuan* adherents practise their movements. Once a very effective deterrent against assailants, it is now practised almost exclusively as a means of keeping fit.

24 Carrots are not just carrots to a Chinese chef. After a bit of work they become birds or dragons. The eyes in the carved carrot dragon on the left light up with power from a small battery hidden inside the vegetable.

and one hole provides play across a deep crevice in the coastline. It is laid out by Robert Trent-Jones, the American course designer and will be 6,800 yards long, par 72. A clubhouse with overnight facilities, a marina, tennis and squash courts, a swimming pool and a health centre are all to be included.

There is some 'spin off' from the project in that promoters have agreed to build four miles of road connecting it to the Kowloon highway system. This will open up currently inaccessible beaches and provide employment and improve communications for villages in the Po Toi-O area. Of course it will also be possible to approach it by sea via the marina.

Hong Kong's fishing season runs from September to the end of March and you will see many anglers trying their luck in reservoirs on the Island, Kowloon, the New Territories and Lantau. Fishing is by rod and line only. Licences cost HK$20 and can be obtained from the Waterworks Department, Leighton Centre, Causeway Bay. A day's catch must not exceed two black bass, two snakeshead and two tilapia. Licence-holders must keep the regulations to the letter, otherwise the angler may be heavily fined.

Water sports are many and there are over 30 beaches. Only in recent years have the Chinese discovered that swimming and underwater exploration can be fun, so not all beaches have changing rooms and showers as yet. Should you see a red flag hoisted anywhere on a beach it means that swimming is dangerous. Repulse Bay is the most popular centre not only because of the beautiful surroundings but because conditions there are suitable for water skiing, wind-surfing, swimming and even paddling. It is most accessible from Central District and a number 6 bus takes you there in half an hour. Seaview has changing lockers and showers and, if you have forgotten your bathing gear, you can hire what you need. Shek O beach on the eastern side of Hong Kong Island can be reached by taking the tram marked 'Shaukiwan' to the end of the line and then catching a number 9 bus. This is also about half an hour's ride.

Of course at any time of the year it is pleasurable to hire a sampan at Causeway Bay or Aberdeen. It is somewhat difficult to go sailing but you can always hire a Chinese junk and crew. Keen sailors who belong to yacht clubs in the United Kingdom should contact the Royal Hong Kong Yacht Club near the Excelsior Hotel to see if reciprocal arrangements exist with their own club. At least they may be able to crew in a race.

8 Macau

Only 40 miles across the sea and linked to Hong Kong by hydrofoil and ferry lies tiny, romantic Macau. It is not just another island in the Pearl River Delta but, like Hong Kong, consists of a peninsula with only two islands instead of many. The peninsula itself is some 2 square miles (5 sq. km) in extent and it is joined to its islands, Taipa and Coloane, by a bridge and causeway. Because it has no airstrip it has an amusing vendetta with Hong Kong, calling it 'Our Airport'. Hong Kong, not to be outdone, refers to Macau as 'one of our tourist attractions'.

Among the many possible derivations of the name Macau there are several linking it with the temple of A Ma or Ma Kok Miu, meaning the goddess of the Sea. According to stories of the past, a poor fishergirl wished to go to Canton and was refused passage by all ships except a small fishing boat. A terrible storm arose after the ships went to sea and all were lost except the fishing boat. It returned safely to Macau guided by the girl A Ma. Legend has it that she walked to the summit of Barra Hill, where the temple is situated, and then vanished. Actually the temple is a complex of small temples rising in a series of individual charming pavilions up the hillside and in one you will find a coloured stone bas-relief of a Chinese junk symbolising the fishing boat. According to the Chinese calendar, for three days in April or May, the boat people of Macau come on pilgrimage to the temple.

A more factual explanation is as follows. When Portuguese sailors first landed in the area, near the thriving A-Ma Temple, they inquired the name of the place and were told it was A-Ma-Gau. Although the Chinese name means the 'Bay of A-Ma' it was adopted as the name of the new settlement, which was known by various spellings in its early days but was usually Amacao. It was later shortened to Macao and more recently the spelling was changed to Macau.

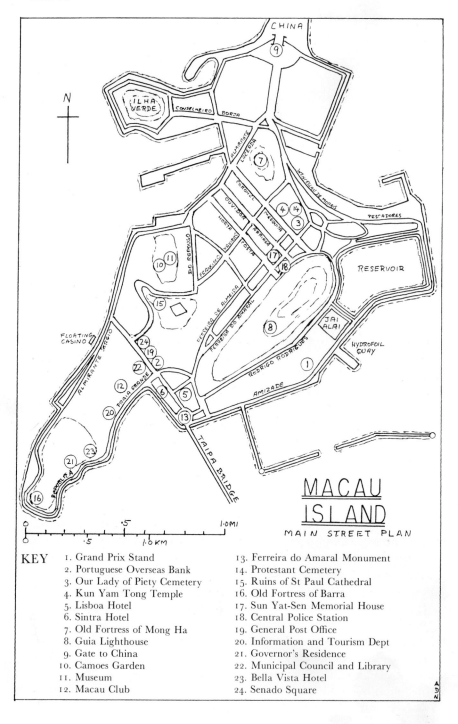

MACAU
ISLAND
MAIN STREET PLAN

KEY

1. Grand Prix Stand
2. Portuguese Overseas Bank
3. Our Lady of Piety Cemetery
4. Kun Yam Tong Temple
5. Lisboa Hotel
6. Sintra Hotel
7. Old Fortress of Mong Ha
8. Guia Lighthouse
9. Gate to China
10. Camoes Garden
11. Museum
12. Macau Club
13. Ferreira do Amaral Monument
14. Protestant Cemetery
15. Ruins of St Paul Cathedral
16. Old Fortress of Barra
17. Sun Yat-Sen Memorial House
18. Central Police Station
19. General Post Office
20. Information and Tourism Dept
21. Governor's Residence
22. Municipal Council and Library
23. Bella Vista Hotel
24. Senado Square

The Portuguese were granted the right to settle in Macau during the remarkable era of exploration by western powers in the sixteenth century. This enviable accolade was bestowed on them by the Chinese for being mainly responsible for stamping out the piracy rampant at the time in the South China Seas. Consequently, Portugal can rightly claim to be the first western power to have gained a firm foothold in the Far East. The Dutch, amongst others, tried to oust her several times, but even during the 60-year period in the seventeenth century when Portugal was occupied by the Spanish, the Portuguese flag continued to fly in Macau. It was after this period that Macau was given its full name which is 'City of the Name of God, Macau. There is none more loyal'.

In 1802, by a quirk of fate, and again in 1808, Macau was occupied by the British as a precaution against seizure by the French! Macau signed a commercial treaty with China in 1887. This stated that China confirmed perpetual occupation and government by Portugal and the latter agreed never to alienate Macau and its dependencies without the consent of China. Further arrangements were made that Chinese Imperial Customs were able to collect duties on vessels trading with Macau. The revenue was an excellent one, particularly when cargoes of opium arrived. The colony has remained under the Portuguese for the last four centuries. The only difference today is that it is no longer considered a Portuguese colony but a territory administered by Portugal.

The Macau governor is appointed by the President of the Portuguese Republic. The principal governing body is a Legislative Assembly of 17 members, 12 of them being elected (six by public vote and six through local associations) and the remainder being appointed by the Governor.

The total population is estimated to be over 350,000 with 3 per cent living on the islands while 5 per cent live on board fishing junks; 95 per cent of the population is Chinese, 3 per cent Portuguese and Europeans, and 2 per cent others. Portuguese is the official language while Cantonese is the most widely spoken. English is Macau's 'third language' and is generally used in trade and commerce.

Although built on seven hills like the great cities of Rome and Lisbon, Macau, perhaps because of its size and distance from Europe, retains its old-time tranquility. This is particularly noticeable when arriving from the stirring activity of Hong Kong. There are ancient forts, quiet squares of faded, yet colourful colonial buildings, flat-roofed houses, cobbled streets and tree-shaded avenues. There is the old-fashioned pleasure of shopping slowly and dawdling over purchases without the jangling of telephones or resigned, queueing people at cash registers. You can stroll across many streets without going through madly rushing traffic. Save for old-timers or newly-arrived gamblers, nobody appears to have frayed nerves. It seemed to me to give the same feeling of slipping back in time as when I stepped ashore off a ferry in Gozo, the sister island of Malta – also, incidentally, built on seven hills!

Going to Macau on a sunny day is a pleasant trip. You leave from the Macau Ferry Pier on Hong Kong Island, where every passenger is charged a small embarkation tax by the Hong Kong Government. Jetfoils are the most comfortable way to travel: they have aircraft seating, are air-conditioned, and have large picture windows. They cruise at more than 40 knots and cover the 40-mile journey in just under an hour. There are over 20 round trips a day and several at night.

Hydrofoils are somewhat slower, and are less stable and less comfortable, but passengers can use the open after deck for a breezy ride or picture-taking. The journey takes about 75 minutes. By the time this book is published a hover-ferry service will also be travelling the route daily. If you prefer slow sea crossings there are always the ordinary ship ferries which take two and a half to three hours to do the crossing. Visas may be obtained for a small sum on arrival.

Macau is definitely a place for cycling or walking, indeed there are no hire cars, which is perhaps just as well as even private ones have difficulty in parking. Taxis are painted black with cream-coloured roofs. They have meters and are reasonable in price. Buses run from 7 a.m. to midnight on all routes within the city, the fare is 50 avos per journey but more for visits to the islands. There is a bus (Route 3) that provides a regular service between the city and the hydrofoil piers for incoming or outgoing visitors. There is a bus stop near the statue of Governor Ferreira do Amaral, just in front of the main entrance of Hotel Lisboa and near the bridge. In summer, you can enjoy a comfortable trip to the picturesque islands aboard a double-deck bus which runs most of the time with the top deck open.

Pedicabs are available and much nicer than the old-time rickshaw. A pedicab is really a tricycle with seating for two passengers and is also known as a 'trishaw'. Your driver can change gear as he peddles along. My advice is: avoid the hills and negotiate the fare in advance.

Macau currency is quickly understood. The pataca (composed of 100 avos) is the official unit and is available in coins and banknotes in denominations of 10-, 20- and 50-avo coins, 1- and 5-pataca coins and banknotes of 5, 10, 50, 100 and 500 patacas. The Macau pataca is

25 Pedi-car for hire in Macau.

pegged by the Government to the Hong Kong dollar, which also circulates freely. Exchange facilities are available at the banks or money changers in the city. On the subject of currency, it is interesting to know that gold was one of Macau's main commercial props. After the Second World War, in 1946, many countries signed the Bretton Woods Agreement forbidding the importation of gold for private use. Portugal did not, and as a result, Macau's gold trade flourished. It was operated through a syndicate which paid taxes to the government. Inevitably, tourists are intrigued by the lovely jewellery especially pieces made of gold. Many of the goldsmiths and jewellers have collaborated with the Department of Tourism to produce a guide listing a number of shops. These are certified by a label displayed on their windows and an official certificate, and quality is controlled. Prices depend on the fluctuating value of gold.

Aside from the attraction of the duty free shopping, two other pillars of the establishment are the churches and casinos, each with mutual disregard for the other. There is complete freedom of worship in Macau. The main religions are Buddhism, Catholicism and Protestantism. To the gamblers, the festive ring is not the church bells but the jingle of coins falling from slot machines as they pay out. The Three Great Kings of Orient take second place to the four kings in a pack of cards. The Chinese are renowned the world over as great gamblers but Hong Kong has decided to outlaw casinos although it allows horse racing. Consequently, to get some variety into losing their money, the people of Hong Kong have to take a trip across the Pearl River estuary and this they do in full measure.

Almost the first thing you see on landing at Macau is the Jai Alai Palace where, in addition to watching the fastest ball game in the world (Jai Alai also known as Pelota Basca), you can enjoy casino facilities. Other famous gambling places are the Casino Hotel Lisboa, the Macau Palace Floating Casino and the Kam Pek Casino (Chinese games only). The gambling concession is operated by a syndicate who pay a percentage of their profits to the authorities and are required to undertake certain public works. Baccarat, Blackjack, Roulette and Boule are played together with some games peculiar to the Chinese such as Fan Tan, Big and Small and Keno and of course there are plenty of 'One-Armed Bandits'!

You can book for all kinds of tours from your hotel. The 'must' above all other buildings to see is the Basilica of St Paul. Not even a shell of its former self (because it was burnt down during an horrific typhoon in 1835) but, of all cathedral ruins, it is one of the most splendid. First of all there is its magnificent site on a hill overlooking the city. Although consumed by fire its whole baroque façade remains intact save for empty windows. It can be reached by climbing a long flight of stone steps edged on the right side by a patterned cobblestone walkway. St Paul's Cathedral was designed by an Italian Jesuit in the early sixteenth century and was built by local Chinese craftsmen and Japanese Christian artisans who had fled from persecution in Nagasaki. Evening visitors gaze up at the ruin in astonishment, for no stained glass could be as beautiful as the sky appears through the empty frames at sunset. The sight is equally lovely on moonlit nights or when clouds scud across the blue sky. Four tiers of ionic pillars reach upward. You can see angels carrying the cross on one level and niches contain statues of saints and decorations, including the chrysanthemum. The chrysanthemum is the flower of Japan and denotes purity. There is a devil in woman's clothing and beneath, in Chinese, an inscription reads 'The devil tempts man to sin'! Tufts of grass and moss add colour and soften broken brickwork. Birds build nests in crevices and fly around the soaring capitals. Tourists kneel on the stairway to take photographs of the ruin to try and catch its glory. Pictures of St Paul's façade grace as many book covers as the little mermaid does Danish books.

The Luis de Camoes Museum was the headquarters of the British East India Company for many years. Built in the 1770s the gracious white building has a central entrance up a wide flight of stairs. It was designed for Manoel Pereira for his retirement after serving the Portuguese king as Comptroller of the Royal Household. At the end of the century it was rented to the august British East India Company who were forbidden, like other foreigners, to own property in Macau. The company, formed by Elizabeth I to manage Britain's trade in the Far East, stayed there for 60 years. It was only allowed to do business in Canton during six months of the year and so its senior personnel spent the six remaining months in Macau and in this way controlled much of the trade with Europe.

Today the Luis de Camoes Museum still retains the air of a country mansion with its lovely gardens which might be in Portugal itself. It seems a most suitable place to display Macau's historic treasures. You walk through a series of white walled rooms, a few with enticing moon door entrances, which are full of exhibits. One room contains several glass cases of beautifully sculptured Chinese horses. There are paintings and engravings of old Macau, Portuguese colonial furniture, exquisite fans, seals and Chinese scrolls, bronzeware, including a magnificent drum of the Han dynasty, pottery and Chien Lung, Ching and Ming porcelain. One room has flooring of old Portuguese

26 Ruins of St Paul's Cathedral in Macau

tiles in a charming, intricate design. In the centre of the musuem you suddenly come upon a well; white brickwork surrounds it and a bucket is suspended on a rope above. Strange to see today, but in times of seige long ago, how useful! Also exhibited is a case containing tiny, embroidered shoes 2 to 3 inches (50 to 75 mm) long, which were worn by Chinese ladies of the aristocracy when the binding of feet was the fashion of the day.

Luis Vaz de Camoes, the most famous of Portuguese poets, after whom the museum is named has another well-known place named after him, the Camoes Garden and Grotto on a hill adjacent to the museum. Here you can see a bronze bust of the poet on a plinth. It was in Macau that he is thought to have written part of his greatest epic poem *Os Lusiadas*. Mystery always clings to such a controversial figure; four cities dispute the honour of being his birthplace in Portugal, Lisbon being one of them. He adored the capital and it was there that he first met the great love of his life, Catherina de Ataide, a lady-in-waiting to the Queen. Hot headed as a young man, he was banished from Lisbon because of outspoken satires on the famous. Although allowed to return to the city later, he still could not curb his temperament and was jailed for joining his friends in a duelling affray. Added to this he had not learned to control his pen and once again abusive satires appeared and he was exiled in 1553.

Even in Goa, Camoes let his pen have full rein on the local personalities and so, for the third time, he was exiled – this time to Macau. Books and essays have been written about Camoes's tempestuous life, based on fact for the most part, but often exaggerated. He fought in many battles (indeed he lost an eye in one), was shipwrecked, travelled widely and was always either greatly admired or detested.

In 1571 the *Lusiadas* was published and presented to King Sebastian. Shortly afterwards the King gave Camoes a pension and his pen brought fame. Phillip II was said to have read and admired it. One of his ministers was heard to remark that it had only one defect; it was not short enough to learn by heart, nor long enough to have no ending!

Do not leave the museum or grotto, if you have a little time to spare, without seeing the old protestant cemetery where many famous people are buried. George Chinnery, an artist of the eighteenth century who lived in Macau, Dr Robert Morrison who translated the Bible into Chinese and also compiled the first English-Chinese dictionary and Captain Lord John Spencer Churchill, Commander of H.M.S. *Druid* and an ancestor of Winston Churchill. This garden-cemetery is next to the museum. For entry you knock at a door which has a plaque overhead stating that it is the Protestant church and cemetery of the English East India Company.

The Leal Senado (literally translated 'Loyal Senate'), built in 1876, is the Town Hall with municipal offices and an impressive Council Chamber. It also contains the National Library, shortly to be transferred to a new site and said to be the oldest European library in the Far East with some 40,000 books, many dating back to the sixteenth and seventeenth centuries. There are mahogany tables, leather, brass-studded chairs, the smell of old manuscripts and the sort of tranquil atmosphere that makes people whisper. The quiet garden with a fountain at the back can be entered by a passageway through wrought iron gates. There once again you are reminded of Camoes, for there is another bust of him amid the flower beds, together with that of the poet Joao de Dues.

From the founding of Macau in 1557 until 1833, the Leal Senado administered the city. From that date the Governor was given stronger powers and the Senate became a municipal authority. The present building dates from the late 1700s and is open to the public from 9 a.m. to noon and 2 p.m. to 5.30 p.m. on weekdays and 9 a.m. to 12.30 on Saturdays.

Across the main street from the Leal Senado is a grey colonial-style building with a tower. This is the Central Post Office and hub of international communications. The postal authorities have recently started issuing special Macau stamps which are available here.

Next to the Post Office is the two-storey, white-washed head-quarters of the city's leading charity, the Holy House of Mercy, which was set up in 1560 by the first Bishop and is now the oldest western charity in Asia. The building dates from the late 1700s but, like the Leal Senado, its façade was added last century. Santa Casa has a long and honourable history and still continues its humanitarian work. The board room on the first floor is open to the public on request and contains portraits of some of the benefactors. Among them Dom Belchior Carneiro, whose skull is preserved in a reliquary, and Marta Merope who left large sums of money when she died in 1829.

The church of St Dominic faces the small square of Largo do Senado and is one of the city's most historic churches. Originally founded in 1582, it is regarded as one of the most beautiful baroque buildings in Macau. It has been the scene of some violent incidents in its time: in 1642 a mob cornered an army officer there and killed him as he sought sanctuary during Mass; in 1704 the prior of a nearby convent was murdered by his own priests; in 1712 there was fighting in the nave between soldiers and priests over the Rites controversy.

The cathedral is behind the Post Office and Santa Casa and dates only from 1937, though built on the site of previous ones. The stone cross in Largo da Se was erected in 1623. The cathedral is noted for its stained glass, Easter festivities and the annual procession of Our Lord of Passos.

The Lisboa Hotel is a great landmark as well as being an enormous

27 A cobbled street in Macau.

building, with several restaurants, shops, three nightclubs, bowling alleys, sauna and swimming pool. The first sight of it makes you think of Las Vegas. It seems to me to look like a great pineapple, but it has been described as 'a helicopter landing on an artichoke' and by another writer as a 'giant ornate marmalade jar.' Yet inside, its 600 rooms and suites are attractively designed.

In contrast, the decor of the casinos is in keeping with the American style rather than the more discreet European atmosphere. One has a vast, rounded chandelier covering most of the bronze sculptured ceiling which is so bright it dazzles the eyes. However, this does not affect the crowds encircling the gambling tables – sometimes three deep – whose eyes follow the quickly moving games that go on 24 hours a day. Money and chips change hands quickly and there is a constant clicking noise. Dress is informal. More men do not wear ties than do. Yet now and then sparkling jewellery and attractive dresses can be seen weaving through the crowds. Whiffs of perfume dilute the thin blue veil of cigarette smoke that hovers over everything. Impassive faces do not give away any secrets and there is always an atmosphere of intensity.

Tempting boutiques and little shops on a higher level surround the casino. The gold jewellery is particularly enticing if you have just won at the tables. There are charms and ornaments of exquisite workman-ship in the form of small horses and dragons, also appropriately, dice – but remember why there are pawn shops galore in the town.

The hotel offers delicious food of all kinds. Japan's most renowned restaurant chain, Furusato, has a branch in the hotel. Here you can enjoy *sukiyaki*, *tempura*, and *sushi* in tatami-matted alcoves.

Caesar's Palace Grill linking the hotel to its two casinos must be visited, if not for its delicious food at least to see part of the decor. One wall between the restaurant and the corridor consists of two sheets of glass the space between filled with water in which shoals of silver and gold carp dart and curve continually. The lighting gives a magical touch.

As well as the Portuguese and Chinese restaurants, there is the A Galera, in the style of an ancient galleon, but food can be forgotten when you see some of the real treasures of the Lisboa: two carved ivory ships in full sail about three feet high minutely equipped and manned; also the most exquisite replicas of two Egyptian Tutankha-men thrones covered in gold leaf. Perhaps the best way to describe this exotic unusual hotel is to quote from its own publicity: 'Other cities have hotels. Macau has the Lisboa.'

From the hotel you look out over the bay and the Praia Grande, a pleasant semi-circular promenade along the sea, shaded by large banyan trees and with benches here and there. Unfortunately cars park along it also but there is still room to walk. You can watch fishermen casting their nets and glance quickly into their buckets to see the catch. Sometimes they play chess on the waist-high wall. If you can drag your eyes from the sea views and look into the parked cars you will notice that most have a little clip inside the front near the mirror which is used to carry refreshing bottles of eau de cologne. On the other side of the road lie charming old houses. Along this way you will see the Bishop's Palace, the faded pink walls of Government House and nearby those of the Governor's home. As you walk along the land rises to a promontory on which is a hotel, the Bella Vista. If you climb up to this you will be rewarded with splendid views. The hotel itself is over a century old and Portuguese tiles cover much of the flooring. A wide granite staircase, the steps lined with plants, leads to the first floor which has a pillared gallery.

Located on the Avenida da Amizada not far from the Lisboa is the 340-room first class Hotel Presidente. Costing US$10 million this 19-storey building is one of the latest hotel additions in Macau. It has two restaurants, boutiques, a beauty salon and coffee shop. The opening ceremony in 1982, performed by Governor Almeida e Costa, was a Sino-Portuguese affair with lion dancers and fado singers.

In keeping with the desire to retain historic monuments and landmarks the 23-room Pousada de Santiago has been built within the walls of the sixteenth-century fortress of Santiago da Barra. Furniture was imported from Portugal to enhance the traditional style of this quiet inn.

If you take the Lisboa as a starting point again, you cross over the road to the Hotel Sintra, on Avenida do Amizade. This hotel is fairly new and moderately priced with 200 rooms. It has a 24-hour coffee shop and a night club. If you walk around the corner from the hotel you will find yourself in one of the main shopping streets, Avenida da Almeida Ribeiro, and others branch out from this on either side until you come to the inner harbour. There are several restaurants on the way, one of the best Cantonese ones being the Palace. Another is the Solmar Restaurant, one of the most popular, with seafood at its best and delicious soups and Portuguese dishes. Almost every Portuguese wine is available from its well-stocked bar. Henri's Galley is on Avenida da Republica along the Praia Grande; here the African chicken is delicious and served with an unusual fried rice. African chicken is a speciality of Macau. The meat is grilled and seasoned with spices, ground coconut and chillies and, as I was often told, many other things. Whatever the ingredients it is a succulent dish. Prawns are also baked or grilled with chillies and peppers. Sardines and other fish come from the fertile Pearl River. Macau is famous for its sole and large juicy prawns. Local game includes quail, pigeon and duck.

All kinds of Chinese food are available: Cantonese, Chiu Chau and northern Chinese cuisine. The Chinese tea served in Macau as usual is

28 The Lisboa hotel in Macau.

perfect and, by chance, as a gambler would say, some has gone down not by drinking but in American history. In 1773 Bostonians were annoyed by the 'English Tea Act' which added stiff taxes to imports. When the British refused to take the tea back, several citizens dressed as Red Indians, crept aboard three of the ships and emptied the cargoes into the harbour. This episode has gone down in history as the 'Boston Tea Party'. The tea had come direct from Macau. A small glass flagon of it, saved at the time, was presented to the Boston Museum and can still be seen today.

One of the delights for the wine-lover coming to Macau is the Portuguese wine, obtained at reasonable prices. Perhaps the best of all Portuguese wine comes from Oporto. Although vintage port matures in the bottle for 20 years or more and is unequalled, its younger rival, tawny port, matured in the cask is also pleasing. The connoisseur will prefer it to ruby port which is a blend of various vintages. In contrast to this after-dinner drink, a white port is often served as an aperitif. From the Portuguese island of Madeira comes the wine of that name in several distinct styles, together with much of their brandy. Gaze into a wine shop window and you will see that a bottle of the best sherry or an ordinary port will cost the equivalent of £3, Chivas Regal whisky £8 while Mateus Rosé, well-known in England for its taste and its distinctive bottle, is less than £3. Other Portuguese wines available include Casal Garcia, Lagosta and some of the Dao reds. To return to more mundane drinks, mineral water can be had at the various hotels and shops. Water is pumped from mainland China and if there is not a bottle of distilled water in your bedroom there will certainly be a thermos of cold boiled water or hot tea.

The teahouse used to be the most popular gathering place in the old days and in Rua 5 de Outubro close to the wharves of the inner harbour, is the Loc Koc, almost a century old and still retaining the authentic atmosphere of long ago. It occupies three floors and the bottom two are typical of local cheap dining rooms. The traditional teahouse is on the top floor with its Chinese decor including a gaily painted ceiling with pyramidal vaulting. It is open from 4 a.m. until mid afternoon, the types of customer varying with the time of day. In the early morning come the fishermen then market workers, bird fanciers with their caged pets, housewives, office staff for lunch and finally young couples for tea.

Moored at the Inner Harbour at the end of the Avenida da Almeida Ribeiro is the extraordinary Floating Casino, known to the local Chinese as the Pirate Ship. Once a restaurant in Aberdeen

Harbour, it was towed from Hong Kong to its present position and redecorated and painted. Its vivid yellows and browns glitter in the sunlight and its ornate pillared decks and colourful parasol awnings draw the eye. Of its three decks the lower two are for gambling and the top one acts as a spacious restaurant. From the latter you get views over the harbour to mainland China.

Greyhound racing is a passion in Macau and the fine strings of dogs are imported from Australia. Races are held at weekends, public holidays and during the summer on the second and fourth Wednesdays of each month. These take place at the Canidrome on Avenue General Castelo Branco. There are bar, snack bar and restaurant facilities. There is also horse trotting on Taipa Island, and one of the most exciting events during the year is the Grand Prix motor race each November.

Sadly the growth of tourism often means many historical buildings and sites vanish and hotels and high-rise offices go up in their place. Fortunately, Macau is making an effort to preserve as much of its heritage as possible. A team of experts from the U.S. came to help study the situation and a 'Heritage Committee' has now been formed which has already accomplished much.

A row of old private buildings that was originally planned to be demolished was taken over, restored, and now houses sections of the Education and Culture departments as well as the Archives and National Library. One army barracks has been turned into a police training school and another into a tourism training school. The black and white cobbled patterned pavements as in front of the town hall, have been left intact. A new theatre is to be built but happily the old Dom Pedro V Theatre has been completely renovated. The portico entrance, its pediment supported by ionic pillars, remains a landmark of Old Macau. The theatre houses the Macau Club said to be the oldest exclusively male club in the Far East. The writer, Austin Coates, once said that were it to be refurbished, the room would rank with the finest in Venice and the Manuel in Vallaspa, and now his wish has come true.

The Sun Yat Sen Memorial House is not the original one he lived in, for that was used to store arms after his death and it blew up some years ago. The new one is close by and very pleasant it is with its front garden where there is a statue of the doctor. He practised medicine in Macau for some years. The house has three floors the first two with pillared verandas and the top floor surrounded by a balcony. The rooms are spacious and high ceilinged. The first one you enter is a reception room surrounded with chairs and couches. The others on

29 The Floating Casino in Macau.

128

30 The Sun Yat Sen Memorial House in Macau.

the ground floor are empty, save for a few glass cases with mementos and flags, but the walls are covered in photographs of the great man. Dr Sun's birthplace was just across the border in Zhongan County and is a popular stop on the China day tours from Macau.

When seen from a distance, the Guia Fortress and the lighthouse on the highest hill in Macau seem like a small settlement. A chapel, turrets and walls built in the seventeenth century add to the illusion. First lit in 1865 the lighthouse is claimed to be the oldest on the China Coast. After being a restricted military area for several years, the small cluster of buildings is now open to the public. A miracle is supposed to have occurred at the chapel. It is said that in 1622, when the Dutch made an attack, the Virgin Mary came outside the chapel and, holding her flowing robe out to each side, deflected bullets aimed at the defenders.

Of the many churches in Macau, only a few can be mentioned here. Each is different and interesting and all have their individual stories and backgrounds. Macau acted as a gateway for Christianity to China and Japan and the reason why there are churches of so many denominations is that all the proselytising nations wished to be seen to be doing good missionary work. There is the church of St Joseph, founded by the Jesuits in 1728 which is reached through its Seminary where missionary students studied before continuing to China. It used to house a precious relic, the bone of St Francis Xavier one of the founder members of the Jesuits, but this has now been moved to the Chapel of St Francis Xavier on the island of Coloane. Also worth a visit is the church of St Augustine, built by the Spanish Augustinian Order. An image of Christ was presented to it in about 1587, and despite several attempts to move the image at a later date to the cathedral or to other churches, it kept on returning mysteriously to St Augustine's. This legend is revived annually in the solemn procession of Our Lord of Passos when the image is paraded to and from the cathedral.

A temple that will appeal to American visitors is the Kun Iam Tong, a fifteenth century Buddhist one with a historic stone table. On it a treaty signing ceremony took place, the first between America and China. It was signed by Viceroy Yi and Caleb Cushing in 1844 declaring 'perfect, permanent and universal peace' between the two countries.

The Kun Iam Tong temple is entered through an ornate entrance to a great hall where three buddhas, representing the past, present and future, stare at you with steadfast eyes. The next hall has the Buddha of Longevity. Succeeding halls have other buddhas and goddesses lit by candles and hundreds of joss sticks, but perhaps most impressive of all are the pavilions themselves, each complete within itself with stone benches, little tables, flower beds, hedges, shrubs and trees. Birds twitter and rustle the leaves, stone cranes, lions and peacocks look at you complacently; then there is the 'Sweetheart Tree' with its gnarled trunks under which lovers pray they will know happiness and remain together.

As you climb up the steps to the various pavilions, near the top one you can look over a wall into the Old Roman Catholic Cemetery where huge sarcophagus graves and various monuments are separated by neat pathways and flower beds. On a summer's day the air is filled with the scent of flowers and a peaceful atmosphere hangs over everything, until you step out through the temple gates again into the noisy city.

The Macau/People's Republic of China border, was officially opened to foreign tourists on 15th October, 1979 and since then an increasing number of visitors have crossed back and forth. There are day tours, or longer ones, organised by travel agents. If you just want to visit the barrier gate you can see the five-starred Red Flag of mainland China flying and perhaps a guard now and them. Photography is now allowed.

While in Macau in 1982 my husband and I saw such a cheerful group of people near the Lisboa that we stopped to enquire the cause of their happiness. A young man broke away from the group and rushed up to us holding out a camera. 'Please take a picture of us with this' he said 'it is the first time we as a family have been together for ten years'. There were six adults and three children in the little group. Not only did Tony take their picture but it is in this book, a change from the usual sad refugee story. The young man with the camera had fled to Indonesia with his brother and both had prospered – so much so that they had returned to Macau and invited the family they had left behind to come from China for the day, for a reunion.

A long bridge and causeway now links Macau with the offshore islands of Coloane and Taipa. After the façade of St Paul's cathedral the bridge is the most photographed place in Macau because it is elegantly arched to allow shipping to pass beneath. It is one mile long, while Taipa is only one and a half square miles itself. Although so small Taipa has many surprising facets. For instance, firecracker factories survive there and very attractive they look, being built one storey high of whitewashed stone with wooden shutters. Then there is the Macau Trotting Club which has opened a new raceway with an oval track, five furlongs in length, a five-storey high stand which can

31 One of the pavilions in Kun Iam temple, Macau.

32 Now that the Macau/People's Republic of China border has been opened to visitors it is possible for the Chinese to come over for a day trip. This particular family had not been reunited for ten years – the text tells their story.

132

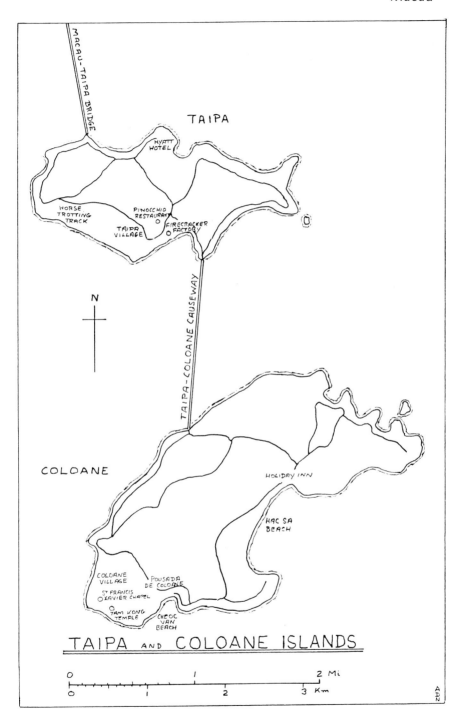

TAIPA AND COLOANE ISLANDS

seat 15,000 spectators and a restaurant catering for 5000. It is the first of its kind in Asia. The University of East Asia is building new facilities there and industry is creeping in. With the opening of the new stadium and the increase in visitors to Taipa, new hotels are being built. There is the Solyar with 400 rooms and the Hyatt Regency. The latter was prefabricated in America and sent out in sections to be erected on the two-acre site. It has 360 rooms and is sited overlooking the Taipa bridge facing towards Macau.

Despite the new tendencies the little village retains its old world atmosphere and among the houses you will find Pinnochio, a famous place to eat. It is slightly hidden in a low row of houses but look out for an ochre-painted frontage with potted plants on the pavement. Try curried crab which is delicious or the roast quail in season. Roast lamb and suckling pig are also specialities, but the latter has to be ordered in advance. The telephone number is 071281.

There are several other places worth a visit in Taipa. To the east of the village is the Church of Our Lady Carmel and the sheltered harbour acted as an anchorage for clipper ships carrying cargoes of opium, silks, tea and other commodities long ago. A Chinese cemetery covers a cliff on the northern side of the island with graves cut into the rock facing the sea. It is regarded as a propitious burial place for Buddhists, Confucians and Taoists.

From Taipa a causeway, built in 1969, leads to Coloane. The island was a pirate's lair at one time with convenient sheltered bays. Also there were pine-covered hills and caves where treasure could be hidden and, save for hunters occasionally coming to shoot quail or pigeon, no one lived there. But today there is a village, roads have been laid out and a power station built. There are small temples and in the local square stands the chapel of St Francis Xavier faced by the Pirate Monument edged with mounds of cannon balls. It was erected to celebrate the defeat of the last pirate raid in 1910.

The chapel, as mentioned earlier, houses the relic of St Francis Xavier, moved there from the church of St Joseph in Macau. It is said to be a bone of his left arm, and is kept in a reliquary on which is inscribed: 'This reliquary was made in London by order of Antonio Pereira and his children, being presented to the church of Macau on 1st September, 1865.' St Francis Xavier, born in 1506 was one of the 15 founder members of the Jesuits and is known in England as the 'Apostle of the Indies'. He was an ascetic and a mystic to whom things spiritual were more real than the visible world, yet he had strong common sense. His missionary work was in the Far East, including Japan, Goa and Malacca. He wished to enter China, and managed to get round the law which then existed excluding foreigners from that empire by persuading the Viceroy of Portuguese India to dispatch an embassy to China. St Francis Xavier died of fever on Sangchuan island near Macau in 1552 having made thousands of conversions during his lifetime, according to his Jesuit biographers. The relic was on its way to Japan in the seventeenth century when the Christians were expelled, so it remains in Macau.

Coloane's clear white sandy beaches have drawn both locals and pleasure seekers since the Second World War. Inns, cafes and picnic areas have appeared but the future promises much more for there is to be a 450-room hotel, country club, casino and an 18-hole golf course in a resort complex facing the shore. This should be open by 1984 and will be only 12 minutes drive from the jetfoil terminal. In anticipation of the expected helicopter service between Hong Kong and Macau it will have its own helicopter pad. The hotel is to be run by the world's biggest hotel chain, Holiday Inn, who plan to have among its recreation facilities two bowling alleys, sauna, health club and two sea-level swimming pools. Among the other attractions there will be a gourmet restaurant serving Portuguese and other western speciality dishes, a Chinese restaurant, a disco and an English pub in the lobby.

Macau shops and other places often close on national holidays and during festivals, so it is as well to know when they occur. However many of the dates are flexible so check with your travel agent. Here are a few that you might like to see.

25th–27th January   *Chinese New Year.*

27th–28th February   A religious spectacle, *The Procession of Our Lord of Passos*. The image of Christ on the cross is taken from the altar of St Augustine's Church in procession to the cathedral where there is a night long vigil before returning it in procession the following day.

5th April   *Ching Ming Festival*. Chinese version of All Saints Day.

16th April   *A Ma Festival.*

13th May   *Procession of Our Lady of Fatima*. A celebration of the religious miracle of Fatima in Portugal in 1917.

6th June   *Dragon Boat Festival*. Dragon boat races take place in the Bay of Praia Grande.

24th June   *Feast of St John the Baptist*. St John is the patron saint of the city and the day is a public holiday.

8th July   *Feast of Na Cha*. At the temple besides the ruins of St Paul's basilica devotees gather to pay homage to their patron. Lion dance takes place through the streets of the city.

12th September   *Mid-Autumn Festival*. Also known as the *Mooncake Festival*.

1st October   National day of the People's Republic of China. A day of firecrackers and dinner parties for much of Macau's Chinese community. Many shops close for the day.

5th October   *Republic Day*. A public holiday to mark the establishment of the Portuguese Republic on 5th October, 1910.

6th October   *Festival of Ancestors (Chung Yeung)*. Prayers are said at hillside graves of ancestors for protection of the coming generation from disaster.

Perhaps it will be the weather that might influence the timing of your visit. The climate in Maccau is moderate to hot, with an average annual temperature of just over 20° Centigrade (68° Fahrenheit) and a yearly mean variation between 16° Centigrade (50° Fahrenheit) and 25° Centigrade (77° Fahrenheit). The humidity is high but seasonal with an average range between 73 per cent and 90 per cent. Rainfall is also high with the yearly total between 40 and 80 inches (100 and 200 cm). The best season is autumn (October to December) when days are sunny and warm, and the humidity is low. The winter (January to March) is cold but sunny. In April, the humidity starts to build up and from May to September the climate is hot and humid with raid and occasional tropical storms (typhoons).

9 Taiwan

Taiwan, situated off the south-eastern coast of the Chinese mainland, has been known in the West for generations as Formosa. The latter name dates back to the sixteenth century when Portuguese mariners, sighting the lovely island from their galleons for the first time, exclaimed, 'Ilha Formosa! Ilha Formosa!' ('Beautiful island! Beautiful island!'). The name Taiwan (meaning 'Terraced Island') goes back further to 1206 when it became a protectorate of the Chinese Empire in the year Genghis Khan founded the Yuan Dynasty. Various colonisers invaded the island by turn; the Dutch, the Spanish, the French. The nineteenth century saw it ceded to Japan and it was only returned to Chinese rule after the Second World War in 1945.

As well as the 240-mile (386-km) long and 85-mile (137-km) wide island, Taiwan territory includes the Pescadores, some 64 small islands 25 miles (40km) to the west. Taiwan's central mountain range is like a mighty spine running from north to south with peaks often soaring more than 10,000 feet. The giant Yushan (Jade Mountain) rises 13,114 feet (4300m) and is the highest in northern Asia. This backbone is offset to the east so that the western side has most of the main roads and railway links. One-third of the country is given over to agriculture and Taiwan's industrial growth in the last three decades has been phenomenal. The population is 17.3 million, the main religions being Buddhism, Confucianism and Taoism. Taipei the capital, with a population of two million, is the fastest growing city in Asia.

We arrived in Taiwan from Hong Kong by China Airlines. This airline is a stranger to the United Kingdom since it does not fly this far west, but it operates two transpacific routes to Los Angeles and San Francisco as well as flights throughout the Far East. It uses the latest types of aircraft on these routes and on its extensive internal networks.

We flew over innumerable rice paddies and fish ponds in bright

Taiwan

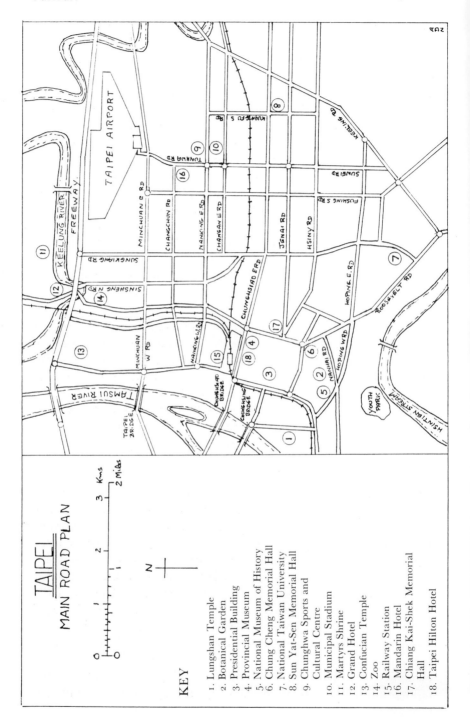

TAIPEI
MAIN ROAD PLAN

KEY

1. Lungshan Temple
2. Botanical Garden
3. Presidential Building
4. Provincial Museum
5. National Museum of History
6. Chung Cheng Memorial Hall
7. National Taiwan University
8. Sun Yat-Sen Memorial Hall
9. Chunghwa Sports and Cultural Centre
10. Municipal Stadium
11. Martyrs Shrine
12. Grand Hotel
13. Confucian Temple
14. Zoo
15. Railway Station
16. Mandarin Hotel
17. Chiang Kai-Shek Memorial Hall
18. Taipei Hilton Hotel

sunlight before arriving at Chiang Kai-shek International Airport some 25 miles (40 km) south-west of Taipei. This modern and spacious airfield has recently taken over the long-haul flights from the older one in Tapei which now handles internal flights only. It can take 5 million passengers and 200,000 tons of freight a year now, and these figures will be doubled by 1990. A freeway provides direct access to the capital and journey time is about 40 minutes.

It seemed only a short time elapsed before we were suddenly surrounded by fast-moving traffic in wide avenues, some lined with palms, and edged on either side by restaurants, shops, hotels, cafes, high-rise flats and office blocks. Traffic is heavy and moves at speed with a large proportion of noisy motorcycles driven with great elan. The combination of vivid colours and the Chinese picture language produces neon signs which are fascinatingly different, if somewhat confusing. Evidence of the buoyant economy is seen on every hand and is emphasised by the cranes, banks, bamboo scaffolding and new buildings which multiply not only in Taipei but in towns all over the island.

At last we climbed a hill which overlooks the city and is surmounted by the almost unbelievable Grand Hotel. It is modelled on the Imperial Palace in Peking and quite unlike any other. The Grand Hotel sprawls over some 20 acres, overlooking the city from the front and the hilly slopes at the back. From balconies at the rear, early mornings provide the unusual sight here and there of graceful figures practising *Tai-Chi*. Adjacent to the hotel, with its tennis courts and swimming pool, is the Yuan Shan Club with more tennis courts and a host of other activities for its members and the guests of the hotel.

The hotel indeed seems like a palace with its enormous, red, multi-coloured lobby. It is surrounded by an ornate balcony above which is a carved wooden ceiling culminating in an imperial dome and hung with lantern chandeliers. A wide staircase leading upward from the lobby to the first floor is edged with carved marble balustrades. Much use is made of Taiwanese marble and hand-made furniture. Leading off the lobby is a restaurant which serves only Chinese food. Elsewhere other restaurants and a coffee shop provide all the usual western fare. Below the lobby is a large shopping arcade linked by parquet walkways. It caters for all tastes and pockets. The hotel's 650 rooms have authentic Chinese decor, combined with television and all the regular facilities. Its vastness means guests would be quite unaware if a convention were being held in the 1500-seat ground floor meeting hall.

Peking is again brought to mind by another building on another hillside, the Martyr's Shrine, a copy of the Hall of Supreme Harmony in Peking's Forbidden City. It honours Taiwan's war dead.

Although Taipei is a modern city now, its name dates back to the Manchu dynasty when it was only a small town surrounded by an 18-foot (5-metre) high wall with four gates built at the points of the compass. The original North gate still remains and the others have been reconstructed. The Presidential Building faces the East Gate and nearby is New Park with its Provincial museum, classical pagodas and gardens. Here again, in the early morning, you can see people practising *Tai-Chi*, quite oblivious of any onlooker. The Botanical Gardens are also close to the Presidential Building and are a blaze of colour with tropical plants and tall palm trees and here too are the National Taiwan Arts Hall, the Central Library and the National Historic Museum.

The most important museum in Taipei, something no visitor should miss as it is one of the finest in the world, is the National Palace Museum. This is in the suburb of Wai Shuang Hsi, north of Taipei, in Yangmingshan (Grass Mountain) Park.

The exhibits, filling some 3000 cases, were brought to Taiwan in 1948 to prevent them falling into the hands of the communists who were overrunning the Chinese mainland. The crates contained the finest pieces amassed in imperial times including porcelain, lacquer and enamel ware, jade and ivory, calligraphy, paintings, scrolls, bronzes and other precious items. Building of the museum started in 1962 in classical Peking style. It was opened on 12th November, 1965 the 99th anniversary of the birth of Dr. Sun Yat-sen, the founder of the Republic of China.

The museum has close to a quarter of a million priceless treasures, but can only display some 3000 at a time, so these are changed every few months. The remainder are carefully packed in crates and stored in a large tunnel burrowed deep into the adjacent, forest-clad hillside. It is of ferroconcrete construction about 180 yards (165 m) long, 10 feet (3 m) wide and 13 feet (4 m) high. It is air-conditioned with an elaborate ventilation system and is connected to the building through a chamber. Very strict security measures are taken when items are moved back and forth.

Jade has always been of great significance to the Chinese. It had its role in ritual worship and Emperors' prayers were carved on jade tablets, put in a jade box and then offered to the Gods. The museum has two sets of these tablets from the T'ang and Sung dynasties.

Of the larger jade pieces I was especially impressed with a screen of

48 panels so delicately carved that it seemed like pale green lace. From the earliest dynasties, the Chinese believed that jade possessed the virtues of holiness and purity. As well as using it for jewellery and ornaments for the enjoyment of the living, exquisitely carved 'funerary' jewellery and articles were placed on the bodies of the dead. Even whole suits of jade panels sewn together were sometimes used to ward off evil and help the deceased enter eternal life, in much the same way the ancient Egyptians used ushabti figures and scarabs. A number of favourite jade items remain permanently on display and it is easy to understand why. Among them is a vase, shaped like a fish, so lifelike it would not seem strange if it leapt out of its glass cabinet. Another is a carving of a lowly cabbage, so real you want to take it in your hand before the dew dries on its leaves.

The museum always has a display of magnificent lacquer work.

Equally spectacular are vessels and other objects in 'Cloisonné' work which, unlike lacquerware, is not made by building up layer upon layer, but by securing thin filaments of silver, gold or copper to a metal base. These hollow designs are then filled with enamel paste of various colours, fired and polished until they gleam in rainbow tints.

The taking of snuff flourished among the aristocracy during the Manchu period and was even believed to be a useful prophylactic against disease. The habit brought into being exquisite snuff bottles and you can see rows of them on display at the museum. Some are of silver, bronze or gold brightly enamelled. Others are of glass, usually round and often made to stand tilted to enable the snuff to be taken out with a small ivory spoon. They are usually painted with flowers, birds or landscapes, sometimes inside as well as out.

Visitors never fail to be astonished at the intricacy of Chinese carving especially on such tiny objects as peach or olive stones and walnuts. One carving is known as the 'Miniature Olive Stone Boat' The subject is taken from the second part of a poem called *Red Cliff* by Su Tong. Su is shown with two friends and a monk as they row out to the Red Cliff. In all there are eight people in this boat; some sitting, some reclining, others drinking or writing poetry. The windows of the boat's cabin can be opened and closed. The artist, Ch'tu Shan, has inscribed the second part of the poem on the bottom of the boat, signed his name and added the year when he carved it – 1737. All of this on one olive stone. Many of these fascinating carvings are so minute that a magnifying glass is placed in the showcase to enable the onlooker to see the fine detail. Some of the ivory carvings are so frail that you feel they would blow away if you breathed on them. A bamboo water-container is delicately wrought in the shape of a lotus leaf gently furled by a breeze. There is a set of 79 wooden cups made with such precision each one fits into the next larger one and you would never imagine that the outer one contains 78 more.

Whole books could be written about the National Palace Museum with its astonishing quarter of a million treasures. Cameras are not permitted within the Museum, but colour slide reproductions of paintings, and replicas of selected masterpieces are available.

The Museum was the idea of President Chiang Kai-shek and the other grandiose building in the city is the magnificent Memorial Hall to his memory. This is in the centre of the city and is as important to Taipei as the Lincoln Memorial is to Washington.

Visitors who climb the wide flight of steps to enter the main hall look across a great expanse of marble flooring and are confronted by the smiling gigantic figure of Chiang Kai-shek. Dressed in a long flowing robe every inch of the 27-foot (9-m) high bronze statue portrays beneficence and dignity. His hands rest on the arms of his chair. He is guarded by two sentries dressed in pale blue uniforms and chromium-plated helmets. They do a one-hour tour of duty when they stand so immobile that you can almost believe that they too are made of bronze. The hourly changing of the guard with its elaborate drill movements delights onlookers.

Two of Chiang Kai-shek's favourite sayings are quoted on the walls behind him, 'To live is to seek a better life for all mankind' and 'The meaning of life lies in the creation of a life beyond life'. The statue dominates the main hall and is bathed in golden light which filters through the sun-like design of stained glass, surrounded by amber and apricot marble, in the cupola above.

Long halls stretch away into the distance and lead through high doorways into various rooms. The main hallway had great bronze vases tastefully arranged with gigantic yellow chrysanthemums when I was there. I was amazed when I walked by them to find that the actual vases were nearly as tall as myself and that the flower arrangements were actually over my head. Exhibits include uniforms and clothing of the late President, documents and portraits. Perhaps one of the most interesting of the latter is a portrait in oils of the President's mother, Madame Chiang Wang. She is wearing a black long sleeved coat edged with fur and has her hands concealed in a matching fur muff.

To me, the most engaging of the many enlarged photographs depicting the President's career was one which shows him and his wife in Egypt, with Roosevelt and Churchill seated between them, in the garden of one of the world's most famous hotels, Mena House. The hotel is over a century old and is built below the only one still standing of the seven wonders of the ancient world – the Great Pyramid of Giza. The picture was dated 1943. This was to be an important year in the annals of Mena House Hotel. Plans for 'Overlord' – the invasion of Europe – had to be discussed by Churchill and Roosevelt, also their proposed meeting with Stalin in Teheran; and future operations in South-East Asia had to be talked over with General Chiang Kai-shek.

A great friend of mine, Lady Joan Coates, told me recently when I said I was writing this book, that her parents, General Sir Chorlton and Lady Spink, had lent Chiang Kai-shek and his wife their villa for this occasion. Roosevelt was in another villa nearby, lent by Mr Casey, Minister of State in the Middle East, where a special ramp was erected to the first floor so that Roosevelt could easily get to his rooms in his wheelchair. In his memoirs Churchill was to write later how Madame Chiang Kai-shek translated for them: 'I had a very pleasant conversation with Madame Chiang Kai-shek and found her a most remarkable and charming personality.' Later Mena House Hotel was to name suites on the first floor after famous people who had stayed there and amongst them were Churchill, Montgomery and Chiang Kai-shek.

A broad boulevard leads from the Memorial Hall edged with parkland fountains and flower beds. Eventually at the far end of this will be an opera house on one side and a concert hall on the other.

When Chiang Kai-shek died, his body lay in state in Dr Sun Yat Sen's Memorial Hall. This is also a most impressive building and has an auditorium capable of seating 2600 people.

Of the many striking temples in Taipei two are outstanding, the Lungshan (Dragon Mountain) temple and the one dedicated to Confucius, the great sage who was born in the year 551 BC. He exercised perhaps more influence upon Chinese culture than any other philosopher. His sayings are quoted all over the world and are as apt today as when they were first uttered by Confucius himself. 'A gentleman', he observed 'takes as much trouble to discover what is right as lesser men take to discover what is wrong.' His advice was given half a millenium before the Christian era.

Lungshan temple is in the oldest part of the city and has been rebuilt at least twice, once after an earthquake in 1816 and again during the Second World War when it was hit by a bomb. Yet today it looks as if it had been there for ever, with its many lovely courts and splendid ornate roof. Local people come and go continually, quite oblivious of tourists. They pray, cajole, give offerings and set flaming

144

33 The entrance to the Chiang Kai-Shek Memorial Hall in Taipei. It was dedicated on 4th April, 1980.

34 Statue of Chiang Kai-Shek in the Memorial Hall in Taipei.

joss sticks in the sand in large bronze bowls. Children play up and down the steps while their relatives say prayers. Stones are tossed into the air to see if they will land a certain way up, thereby foretelling whether supplications will be answered. Meantime the silent gold-leafed buddhas gaze on the scene, Ma Tsu goddess of the Sea and Kuan Yin the goddess of Mercy.

Taipei's shopping district is fascinating and if you only have a little time to spare do not forget to go to the Taiwan Handicraft Centre, 1 Hsuchew Road where the prices are government controlled so you do not need to bargain and everything is clearly marked. On the other hand, if you enjoy bargaining and have plenty of time, it can be fun elsewhere for both parties. Souvenir hunters will not be disappointed. There are miniature and full-size decorative screens, brocaded or beaded slippers, handbags and jackets, coral jewellery and every kind of brass, bronze, lacquer and china ware. Indeed shopping can be, as one of the advertisements says, an exciting adventure! Added to the enjoyment is the fact that shops stay open until 10 o'clock at night.

Taipei hotels are modern and comfortable and a few of the western chains are represented. However, one word of warning. It is advisable to carry the name of your hotel around with you written in Chinese so that a taxi driver who may not speak English will not give you a blank stare when you ask to be driven home. It is also a help if you have any address you want written in Chinese in the same way. Your hotel porter will aid you.

Taipei has numerous restaurants and cafes apart from those in hotels. Most hotels seem to have at least two, one offering Chinese cuisine and the other western food. Perhaps most unusual to the tourists are Mongolian barbecue restaurants. You really cannot go wrong visiting one of these, as you choose your own food. You fill a bowl and add condiments from a refrigerated buffet counter. The inviting spread includes all kinds of meat, poultry and vegetables. When you finish making your choice you hand your bowl to a waiting chef who will then proceed to cook what you have chosen over a piping hot grill, turning bits and pieces over deftly as they sizzle. When it is placed before you the only warning is to remember it is very hot – but oh how delicious! You will find that several restaurants will barbecue meat Peiping style, which means it is cooked at your table.

The Chinese believe that food should not only be pleasing to the palate, but that it is also a work of art. Vegetable sculpture is an example of this and the Taipei Hilton chefs seem to have reached the very peak of perfection in this extremely difficult skill. They have won many prizes and a search was made for more books on the art to see if

35 The interior of the Lungshan Temple in Taiwan.

36 Practising for the Dragon Dance in Taiwan.

there were other ideas. None were available so it was decided that the Hilton should produce its own books – and it has. One is called *Chinese Vegetable Carving* which is full of practical hints, the type of equipment required and all you should know although you could probably never do it! However the pictures are so beautiful you want to frame them and it seems impossible that such lovely things were actually carved out of vegetables. The other book is equally enthralling, called *Culinary Heritage* and, as well as more lovely pictures of vegetable and fruit carvings (imagine a tiny goldfish carved from a lowly carrot!) there are reproductions of ancient scrolls and paintings showing fascinating and sumptuous banqueting. In some, the figures are nodding off to sleep yet looking happy and replete for the Chinese have always been in love with their own cooking – not to mention its presentation.

It was at the Hilton that we met one of the most interesting people on our travels, Julia Chan, who is currently the only lady manager in the Hilton chain. She was born in Hong Kong and joined the Hilton there in 1964 as secretary to the front desk assistant manager. Always interested in food and wine she ultimately became the food and beverage manager. She loved everything to do with food, hot and cold, bland or spicy, sweet or sour, but particularly its presentation; there was only one thing wrong – she was allergic to alcohol.

Julia Chan was not to be deterred by her allergy and, being a perfectionist, decided she was going to overcome this obstacle. She sought advice from her doctor and, for several weeks, each time she tasted a wine to see how it went with the appropriate food, she would visit him the next day for an injection to ward off the inevitable rash. As she seldom took more than a few sips she soon mastered the allergy. Even today, without the injection she rarely takes a whole glass of wine, 'Because', she says, 'My cheeks immediately get faintly flushed. I know you people in Britain have a compliment "cheeks rosy as apples" but it is considered the exact opposite out here. Even a little wine will give a Chinese woman pink cheeks and this is considered to be ugly!'

Julia came to the Taipei Hilton as the banquet manager when it opened in 1973. Now, as overall manager, she has a staff of 750 people in the 700-room hotel, which is noted for its gourmet dishes. We had a rendezvous with this unusual lady in, of all places, the Hilton English pub. It was a setting we were used to, but we had an unusual time. The month was December and suddenly tiny bowls of strawberries appeared with that delicious smell reminiscent of 'fraises du bois'. However they were not these small berries but slightly larger ones cut exactly down the centre so that the small middle vein, shaped like an inverted arrow, was still full of juice.

Only about five minutes walk from the Hilton is Taipei's central station. As soon as you board a Taiwanese train you get the usual attentive but unobtrusive service you find on their aircraft, and it is assumed, of course, that the first thing you would like, at whatever time of day, is a cup of tea. You are given a choice of green, black or jasmine-scented tea, served free of charge. Stewardesses distribute newspapers and magazines, also small wet towels for passengers to refresh themselves. Dining cars offer a variety of dishes both Chinese and Western. If you wish to go to Hualien it takes two and a half hours by train. The flight from Taipei's city airport takes a mere 20 minutes and it is the latter way that is most used by tourists.

Hualien, about halfway up the island's east coast, facing the sea on one side and backed by mountains, is an attractive town. It is from here that you can begin your drive through the amazing Taroko marble gorge said by many to be one of the seven wonders of the modern world. It is part of the East-West Highway which some 10,000 workers took 46 months to build. The price was tremendous for 450 people lost their lives at the task and the cost was over US$11 million. This great effort was to open up Taiwan. It was finished in 1960 and has proved to be worth the financial investment (though not, of course, the loss of human life) not only in industrial development but in farming and logging while also providing an unusual scenic drive. It is 120 miles (190 km) long.

The tourist's interest in visiting the gorge is increased by the possibility of visiting one of the many marble factories. Everything you see is made of marble from the gorge which yields thousands of tons in various colours. You can buy anything from tables to jewellery and all at reasonable prices. Perhaps the prettiest tints are the green and grey ones but the great snag, if you are travelling by air, is the weight. However this does not stop you buying small vases, trinkets and jewellery, all so attractive that the choice is difficult. The factories are of course prepared to ship the heavier items for you.

The eastern entrance to the 12-mile (19-km) long gorge is through a pleasing oriental gateway painted red and gold which almost leads you to expect a luxuriant park on the far side but, as your vehicle snakes up through Swiss-style hairpin bends, the illusion vanishes. There are 38 tunnels along the ravine, their cool darkness leading to more and more striking scenes. Many of the tunnels have openings to provide ventilation and light but which also enable sightseers to glimpse fantastic views, downward to a rushing stream seemingly

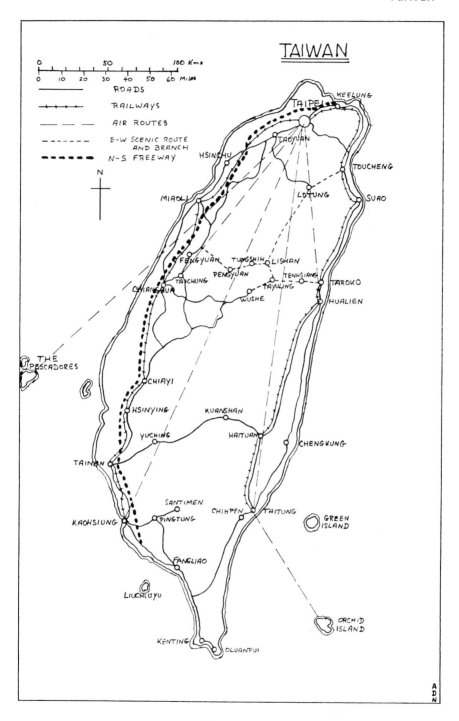

152

37 The Taroko marble gorge in Taiwan, said by many to be one of the seven
wonders of the modern world.

miles below, or upward to sheer marble walls soaring high into the blue sky. In the open sections you find yourself driving through lush scenery with tropical trees and plants. For those who have driven through the Swiss or Austrian Alps it is strange to see similar peaks and hillsides covered not in pine and fir trees or edelweiss but in palms, pear trees, crimson and yellow poinsettias and flowering azeleas in blossom – and all this in the month of December.

Although our visit was so late in the year, the sense of unreality was heightened by the fact that, although we were several thousand feet up, the weather was warm and sunny. Most visitors traverse the gorge by car, bus or motorcycle, though some hardy souls hike the entire length. If you walk into some of the tunnels to admire the views through the openings, beware of passing vehicles whose drivers may have been momentarily affected by the contrasting light between tunnel and daylight.

A visit to the gorge can be combined with a trip to Sun Moon Lake, a year-round resort set in the central mountains among tea plantations. Here you can sail and windsurf. There are attractive pagodas, Buddhist temples and an aboriginal village. The Ami and other tribes give lively song and dance shows in this part of the island which your tour operator can arrange for you to see. However, to return to the Taroko Gorge. We continued along the highway to Lishan (Pear Mountain) a year-round resort 6380 feet (1945 m) above sea level.

We lunched at Lishan House and then visited the local fruit and vegetable market where sellers were attractively dressed in local costume including wide straw hats. The mode of local transport is novel and economical. It consists of a two-wheeled tractor attached to a small truck with a seat for the driver between the two units.

Then we drove to Taichung. This is in the centre of the island and the third largest city in Taiwan. It covers some 60 square miles (160 sq. km) and has a population of about one million. To visitors the climate seems perfect with little rain, plenty of warmth and long sunny days. We had dinner and spent the night at the National Hotel. Two unusual things struck me about our bedroom. One was that as well as a Bible in English by my bedside there was also a Life of Buddha in English and, beneath each bed, a new pair of bedroom slippers – very comfortable after a day's sightseeing.

The following morning we set off for Lukang where there are two important temples, one dedicated to Kuin Vin, goddess of Mercy, and the other to Ma Tsu, goddess of the sea. The latter has a constant flow of pilgrims and we were most fortunate in that as we approached

38 Lishan market, Taiwan.

it there was a ceremonial parade with a dragon in its midst. Firecrackers were let off, costumed men danced and a band played. We were told that this pageant ensured that no evil spirits would invade the temple that particular morning. Onlookers with smiling happy faces courteously made way for us to watch the long procession.

Before leaving Lukang, the Folk Arts Museum is a must if there is a little time to spare. It is housed in two large buildings with 30 rooms and one part is furnished as the house of a wealthy mandarin might have been long ago. You pass through living and banqueting rooms. In the latter an enormous wooden couch at the end of the room was wide enough and deep enough to seat at least a couple of dozen people in comfort if they curled up their legs and sat in rows. There are vintage photographs including ones of well-born ladies with tiny feet which had been bound since birth. You can see exquisite embroidery, basket work, religious vessels, musical instruments and even a small puppet theatre.

One of the loveliest seaside resorts in Taiwan is the National Park of Kenting at the southernmost tip of the island. Situated at the meeting place of the Taiwan (Formosa) Strait, the South China Sea and the Pacific Ocean, its waters abound with exotic fish, coral gardens and scenes which delight scuba divers. A large recreation and vacation area of some 20 square miles (50 sq. km) has been built with fabulous scenery and including strange volcanic formations and bird sanc-tuaries. There is a botanical garden containing hundreds of varieties of trees all labelled in Latin, Chinese and English. Every conceivable tropical flower flourishes here and of them all perhaps the lotus is the most exotic.

Chinese poets have always praised the lotus. In the Sung Dynasty the writer Chou Tun-yi said of it: 'Although it emerges from mud the lotus remains pure and spotless and is verily the quintessence of all flowers'. Another poet has attributed its appearance on earth to direct descent from heaven as a joyful gift to mankind. It has occupied a special place not only among the Chinese: in Pharaonic times, it had symbolic association with the Nile, the giver of life; the Hindus regarded it as an indication of affluence; and, when the legendary Odysseus offered the plant in the course of his wanderings to his sailors, they became lotus-eaters who forgot their homes and only wished to remain on the island where it grew.

The Chinese cherish the lotus not only for its beauty and purity but also as a source of food. The seeds make one of the best sweetmeats of a Chinese feast. The roots are usually sliced and cooked or, if preferred, eaten raw. The leaves are often used as wrappers for boiled or steamed food. Legend has it that Buddha's association with the lotus began at birth when he stepped on five of the flowers. Probably because of this he is depicted in paintings, sculptures and embroideries as seated on a throne of lotuses or standing on a base composed of the flowers. Lotus ponds are to be found everywhere in Taiwan, many of them landscaped in classical Chinese style. Among the more notable ones in Taipei are those in the Botanical Gardens and the grounds of the Sun Yat Sen and Chiang Kai-shek Memorial Halls.

The Taiwanese are as fond of mythical creatures as they are of flowers. Sightseers are often fascinated by the decorations on temple roofs. These usually consist of three mythical creatures, the dragon, the phoenix and the unicorn. The animal they really love however is a mixture of myth and real life, the lion, symbolic of fearless courage, phenomenal strength and unparalleled ferocity. Because of these qualities lions have been considered the ideal guards against intruders and evil spirits. As it was impracticable to have the live variety guarding important buildings, statues are used instead and, because marble is abundant in Taiwan, they are usually made of that long lasting and attractive stone. Marble lions guard the bridges on the east-west, cross-island highway. Tourists often stop to photograph the lion sentinels guarding the Bridge of Motherly Devotion and they are on duty at the Martyr's Shrine and National Palace Museum in Taipei.

Appendix I

PRINCIPAL HOTELS

Note   In each place the Tourist Authority issues complete up-to-date lists which are easily obtainable.

HONG KONG
Island
Mandarin, Connaught Road
Excelsior, Causeway Bay
Hong Kong Hilton, Queen's Road
Furama Intercontinental, Connaught Road
Plaza, Causeway Bay
Lee Garden, Causeway Bay

Kowloon
Peninsula, Salisbury Road
Holiday Inn, Harbour View
Holiday Inn, Golden Mile
Sheraton, Nathan Road
Regent, Salisbury Road
Hyatt Regency, Golden Mile
Royal Garden, Tsimshatsui East
Shangri-La, Tsimshatsui East

TAIWAN
Grand, 1 Chungshan North Road, Sec. 4, Taipei
Taipei Hilton, 38 Chunghsiao West Road, Sec. 1, Taipei
Mandarin, 166 Tunhua Road, Taipei
Holiday Inn, International Airport, Taipei
Holiday Inn, 279 Liuho Road, Kaohsiung

National, 257 Chunghang Road, Sec. 1, Taichung
Lai-Lai Shangri-La, 12 Chungshiao East Road, Taipei
Sun Moon Lake, Sun Moon Lane, Nantou

MACAU
Lisboa, Avenida da Amizade
Presidente, Avenida da Amizade
Sintra, Avenida Dom Joao IV
Pousada de Sao Tiago, Avenida da Republica
Holiday Inn, Coloane Island ⎫
⎬ *(under construction at time of writing).*
Hyatt Regency, Taipa Island ⎭

Appendix II

USEFUL WORDS AND EXPRESSIONS

English	Chinese phonetic pronunciation
Bad	M'ho
Beer	Bay jaoo
Bring me	Ling
Bus	Bar see
Coffee	Gar
Give me	Ling
Good	Ho
Good bye	Joy geen
Good day	Jo sun
Here	Nee
How much	Gay doe sheen
Left	Jao
Listen	Teng
Little	Seeoo
Milk	N'gaoo lie
Money	Cheen
Never mind	M'gon yo
No	M'hi
Not possible	M'haw
Please	Cheng nay
Possible	Haw
Right	Yao
Stop	Ting gee
Street	Guy
Sugar	Tong

Taxi	Taxi
Tea	Char
Thank you	M'goy
That's all	Gao
Too expensive	Ti gwy
Train	Deen chair
Water	Sooey
Why	Deen guy
Yes	Hi

Numerals

0	Ling
1	Yot
2	Ee
3	Sarm
4	Say
5	Ng
6	Look
7	Chut
8	Bort
9	Gaoo
10	Sup

Index